Box 4

Mass Persuasion

The Social Psychology of a War Bond Drive

by

ROBERT K. MERTON

With the Assistance of
MARJORIE FISKE AND ALBERTA CURTIS

GREENWOOD PRESS, PUBLISHERS
WESTPORT, CONNECTICUT

MASS PERSUASION: *The Social Psychology*
of a War Bond Drive

All rights in this book are reserved.
No part of the book may be reproduced in any
manner whatsoever without written permission
except in the case of brief quotations embodied
in critical articles and reviews.

Originally published in 1946 by Harper & Brothers Publishers,
New York and London

This edition is reprinted by arrangement with The Free Press,
a division of The Macmillan Company

Reprinted in 1971 by Greenwood Press, Inc.
51 Riverside Avenue, Westport, CT 06880

Library of Congress catalog card number 77-136076
ISBN 0-8371-5226-7

Printed in the United States of America

10 9 8 7 6 5 4 3 2

To the Memory of
ALFRED S. ETCHEVERRY
Private, Army of the United States

Contents

Preface

PROPAGANDA HAS forced itself upon the attention of twentieth century man. Though it is far from being a new technique of social control, propaganda has taken on such enlarged amplitude and heightened intensity that it has become a source of concern for some and a focus of interest for many.

As a concentrated process of spreading values and ideas, attitudes and beliefs, propaganda is particularly likely to expand and proliferate in times of moral confusion. When values are in flux, when competing parties and factions and interests offer their distinctive ideological goods in the market place of opinion, when a unity of moral outlook has been suddenly shattered or has slowly decomposed into shapeless disagreements, the propagandist has his heyday. And with the growth of propaganda, contemporary social science has come to train its sights upon the several tactics and the over-all strategy of propaganda. An abundance of scientific papers and a small library of specialized books attest this focus of interest.

Since propaganda has become a powerful instrument for either good or evil, more should be known of its workings. This book is yet another effort to add to our stock of knowledge on this score. Its scope is severely limited. It seeks to scale down the investigation of propaganda in the large to the dimensions of a manageable inquiry into a single case of mass persuasion. A radio star succeeded in selling some $39,000,000 of war bonds in the course of one day's broadcasts. Our study asks and seeks to answer one central question: how did this come about? But though we deal with a specific case of mass persuasion, we look also into its general implications, for in observing particulars we inevitably imply universals.

With few exceptions, research has been almost wholly concerned with the content rather than the effects of propaganda. Inquiry in this field has been focused on the appeals and rhetorical devices, the stereotypes and emotive language which made up the propaganda materials. But the actual processes of persuasion have gone largely unexamined or have been matters for speculation rather than research. Although this book does not fully uncover the major mechanisms of mass persuasion, it does, perhaps, advance our knowledge in this respect. At the very least, it seeks to suggest bases for continued investigation of strategic problems.

In genesis and in substance, this book is an outgrowth of collaboration. The initial suggestion for the study—one in a series by the Bureau of Applied Social Research of Columbia University—came from my colleague Professor Paul F. Lazarsfeld, Director of the Bureau and initiator of many pioneering investigations in the field of mass communications.

Miss Marjorie Fiske, former Research Associate of the Bureau, had an indispensable part in the analysis of the data and in the preparation of the report. The design of the investigation was laid out in co-operation with Miss Alberta Curtis, Research Director of Station WNEW, and an alumna of the Bureau, who lent her talents to the initial assembling of the interview materials. Without their collaboration, the study would not have been possible.

During the period of his association with the Bureau, Goodwin Watson contributed valuable editorial suggestions, as did Granville Hicks and Major Theodore Silverstein. For the exceptionally difficult interviewing we are indebted to Lillian Mintz, Joan Doris, Jeannette Green, Helen Kaufman, Carol Coan, Patricia Salter and Alfred Etcheverry. I am grateful to my secretary, Miss Ruby Taylor, for her continued good patience in agreeing to the revision of several drafts of the manuscript.

The errors and flaws which remain despite this generous collaboration are entirely chargeable to me.

R. K. M.

Columbia University
September 1945

In general the whole technique of propaganda, persuasion and public relations needs the most intensive study before the findings of science can be socially applied. When does propaganda defeat its own ends by putting up counter-resistance? What are the relative values of reiteration and variety of appeal? Of the printed word, the cinema, and the radio? Of rational persuasion as against mere suggestibility? Of intellectual comprehension as against a sense of active participation? We do not know, and until we know, our progress toward efficient social structure and a fuller life will be fitful and slow.

—JULIAN HUXLEY

Chapter 1

A CASE OF MASS PERSUASION

IN EVERY age, the artifices of rhetoric have moved men to act—
or to refrain from action. Techniques of persuasion are known
to have a long history and they have, probably, a longer pre-
history. But never before the present day has the quick persuasion of masses of people occurred on such a vast scale. The
trivial and the large decisions alike are made the object of delib-
erate control. Large populations are brought to prefer a given
brand of soap or hair tonic or laxative. Or, predisposed by their
conditions of life, large masses are persuaded to follow a political leader who means many things to many men. Loyalties are
captured and control of mass behavior temporarily ensured.
Masses of men move in paths laid down for them by those who
persuade.

But how does all this come about? What enters into the persuasion of large numbers of people? It is true, and not very revealing, to say that the applications of science and technology
have made it possible. To be sure, the media of mass communication enable large aggregations of people to read, look and
listen. And in exposing themselves to the content of print,
movies and radio, people may become susceptible to their influence. But clearly these media do not explain the character of
mass persuasion. The physical apparatus is a necessary condition, but no more. The processes and techniques of persuasion
must be examined in their own right.

As long as we continue to speculate about the arts of persuasion and propaganda we shall have little to add to what Aristotle, Bacon, Hobbes and Bentham had to say each in his own day. Only by closely studying actual instances of mass persuasion will we come to understand its workings more fully. And perhaps, through studies of cases, we may learn effective defenses against being persuaded in spite of ourselves. This book is about one such case. By viewing it as a specimen of mass persuasion we may be able to learn more about the general problem through the specific instance.

The Case in Hand

September 21, 1943, was War Bond Day for the Columbia Broadcasting System. During a span of eighteen hours—from eight o'clock that morning until two the next morning—a radio star named Kate Smith spoke for a minute or two at repeated intervals. (Stardom implies a mammoth audience: it was estimated that in 1943 some 23,000,000 Americans listened to Smith's daytime programs in a week and some 21,000,000 to her weekly evening program.)

On sixty-five distinct occasions in the course of the day, she begged, cajoled, demanded that her listeners buy war bonds. Within the narrow borders of her brief messages, Smith managed to touch upon a variety of themes enshrined in American culture. She talked of neighbor boys from American towns and villages, now facing danger and death in other lands. And people listened. She told dramatic tales of generosity and sacrifice by soldier and civilian alike. People continued to listen. She invoked themes of love and hate, of large hopes and desperate fears, of honor and shame. Apparently, there was nothing here of a cut-and-dried radio script. This was presented as a personal message, iterated and reiterated in a voice often broken, it seemed, by deep emotion. And people did more than listen.

Before nightfall, Smith could begin to announce large totals of bond pledges. At one climactic moment, she reported that listeners in Los Angeles had that day subscribed several million dollars in response to her appeals. Each succeeding announcement acclaimed a swelling national sum of pledges. By the end of this, her third all-day drive, Smith had shattered her previous bond-selling records. During her first drive, she had amassed a million dollars in pledges and her second had netted two millions. But this Third War Loan appeal far outstripped her earlier efforts, resulting in thirty-nine million dollars of bond pledges in the course of the one day. Here, apparently, was an extraordinary instance of mass persuasion.

Its Research Value

We decided to study the Smith bond drive on the assumption that it would provide a peculiarly instructive case for research into the social psychology of mass persuasion. And so it proved to be. Although her name inevitably recurs time and again throughout the book, this is *not* a study of Kate Smith. Her bond drive merely provides the material for an investigation of the structure and dynamics of mass persuasion in our society.

The Smith bond drive satisfied many requirements of a study in social psychology. It was, first of all, a "real-life" situation rather than a synthetically arranged event. Secondly, the bond purchases provided an index, however crude and tentative, of effective persuasion. Thirdly, the situation was emotionally freighted and many listeners were deeply involved in the interplay of sentiments. In the fourth place, we could readily determine the objective aspects of the situation: we knew precisely what happened in the broadcast. Fifth, the persons whom we studied came from different social groups and were not drawn from a hapless group of college students co-operating under the firm discipline of their instructor. And, finally, our subjects' response to the broadcasts occurred within a well-defined cultural context, which helped clarify the role of persuasion in American society.

By reviewing each of these considerations briefly, we can locate the distinctive advantages and limitations of this body of research materials.

1. *"Real-life" situation*

A review of the literature in social psychology indicates at once that there have been relatively few circumstantial analyses of responses to propaganda in real-life rather than contrived situations. Yet, it is generally conceded that, for fruitful investigation in this field, "experiences which are novel, emotionally charged and realistic (as opposed to laboratory-like) are most effective."[1] The laboratory setting should not differ so markedly from situations in ordinary life as to preclude or vitiate the transference of findings from the laboratory to the world outside.

The laboratory experiment runs the risk of diverse sorts of distortions. Chief among these, as experimenters in social psychology have long been aware, is the danger that subjects' behavior may be distorted by their recognition that they are being subjected to an experiment, particularly when they have some knowledge, real or fancied, of the purpose of the experiment. In such instances, subjects may respond, not only to the presumed experimental variables, but also to the experimenter and the assumed objectives of the experiment. They may seek to behave "properly," that is, in a fashion conducive to the assumed "desired results" or to a socially acceptable performance. Or, contrariwise, they may be somewhat resentful of an imagined assault on their sense of personal autonomy when they

[1] Gardner and Lois B. Murphy and Theodore M. Newcomb, *Experimental Social Psychology* (New York: Harper & Brothers, 1937), p. 979.

are used as "guinea pigs," thus exhibiting resistance to the experimental requirements. The various ways in which these and other distortions are produced by an "artificial" laboratory situation are well known and need not be developed further.

One of the genuine merits then, of the present case is the spontaneous response to the "experimental" stimulus patterns. The responses of listeners to the Smith broadcasts could not, of course, be prejudiced by special reactions to a contrived laboratory situation.[2] Our subjects were not asked to listen to the Smith broadcasts; they did so on their own initiative. The situation was not structured for them by the investigators; they supplied their own setting, their own context for listening. They were not subjected to conditions wholly alien to their usual routine of radio listening. In short, if the fact that the behavior of our "subjects" did not occur under strictly controlled conditions proves a liability for rigorous experimental inquiry, the self definition and "normality" of these conditions proves a distinct asset for an understanding of the concrete workings of radio as a medium for mass persuasion.

2. *Index of effective persuasion*

If we are concerned with the analysis of mass persuasion, we must first have some means of determining the instances in which such persuasion did and did not occur. Nor is this seemingly self-evident requirement easily met. Social psychology has often found it most difficult to establish valid indices of the effects of propaganda or persuasion. As social psychologists are well aware, such studies must at times deal with behavior that is only remotely related to the psychic variables with which they are actually concerned. Thus, experimental studies of shifts in racial attitudes will often deal, not with the expression

[2] To be sure, comparable biases may have been introduced in the *collection* of our interview data, a possibility which is considered in detail in our later discussion.

of these attitudes in the ordinary routine of daily intercourse or under the provocative circumstances of crisis situations, but with a laboratory situation in which subjects solemnly record their agreements and disagreements with a series of printed statements which allude to a given racial group. The gap between the behavior actually observed and the behavior that is the basic object of the inquiry is at times so great that it is difficult to draw from the experimental findings inferences that can apply to other situations. In short, there is a considerable problem of constructing appropriate indices of the effects of propaganda.

The very nature of the Smith case largely obviates this difficulty. As a preliminary and crude index of effective persuasion —an index which we shall later subject to close scrutiny—we have the fact that certain listeners did and others did not respond to the Smith appeals by the purchase of a war bond. This is not to suggest that this fact "speaks for itself." Some degree of persuasion may have occurred in instances where bonds were not pledged and, contrariwise, some bond pledges may represent only a slight measure of effective persuasion by Smith. Nonetheless, in so far as the bond pledge provides an observable and realistic, if not impeccable, index of persuasion, it facilitates our analysis.

3. *Ego involvement*

A perennial problem facing the experimenter in social psychology is that of ensuring adequate incentives for participation in the experiment. Often, it is difficult to set up experimental goals which will be taken as genuine goals by subjects. Moreover, the experimental situation may tap peripheral rather than central interests. The difficulty of generating strong emotions in the laboratory situation militates against the study of certain types of propaganda and persuasion. The experimental conditions are such as not to evoke deep-lying affect or ego involvement.[3] Subjects may follow the experimenter's instructions and yet not exhibit the appropriate attitudinal or emotional set.

The very character of the Smith broadcasts and the situations in which they were heard largely eliminate this set of problems. This was no synthetic situation involving trivial or superficial experience. The appeals aroused profound emotions and activated strong sentiments: guilt, pity, sympathy, anxieties. There is abundant evidence, as we shall see, that many of our subjects were profoundly stirred by the Smith appeals, that they felt some of their most important values were involved in the experience, that deep-lying sentiments found expression in the context supplied by the broadcasts.

4. *The stimulus pattern*

Many case studies in social psychology must attempt to reconstruct the objective outlines of the stimulus pattern to which subjects were exposed, since there is no ready access to the character of the situation except through the reports of informants. Recent studies of race riots, for example, manifestly could determine the character of the situations in which participants found themselves only through such retrospective reports. These data enable the investigator to discover the *subjective* definitions of the situation but not the actual state of affairs to which people were responding selectively.

In the present instance, we have access to a substantial part

[3] Murphy, Murphy and Newcomb conclude their review of experimental evidence in this field with the following commentary: "After becoming accustomed to the barely significant changes in attitudes so often following experimental procedures, one is forcibly reminded of how unreal most of these procedures are. We give lip service to the fact that attitudes of importance are deep-laid in the fundamental needs of life as molded by group patterns, and then we proceed to experiment with the use of an opaque projector! Experimental ingenuity can surely be expended along the lines of our most important hypotheses." *Op. cit.*, pp. 971-2.

of the objective stimulus patterns, in the form of the messages broadcast by Smith. Obviously, actual recordings of the Smith appeals would have provided a more complete set of material, inasmuch as her voice, as well as the sheer content of her talks, constituted an integral part of the stimulus situation. Lacking such recordings, however, we find that a content analysis of her broadcasts provides us with a fairly systematic account of the themes and symbols to which listeners were responding. Since we are acquainted with what she *actually* said we are in a position to determine the selective (apperceptive) character of the responses of subjects. We can ascertain the foci of interest, the distortions, the selective emphases supplied by subjects, in a fashion which would not be possible if our sole source of information regarding her talks were the reports of our interviewees.

5. *Informants*

From time to time, social psychologists make uneasy comments on the fact that their subjects in experimentation, or case studies, are characteristically drawn from the population of students.[4] In some instances students constitute a peculiarly poor group of subjects not only because they are unrepresentative of the larger population, but because of their comparative familiarity with the general objectives and techniques of psychological experiments. They are, in other words, more likely to respond not only to the assumed experimental stimulus patterns but to the (real or imputed) purposes of the experiment. Moreover, by largely confining subjects to students—drawn from a selected age-grade and educational stratum—the applicability of results to other groups becomes doubtful. It may not be too much to say that an advanced "social psy-

[4] For example, students constituted the subjects in 28 of 34 experiments on the modification of social attitudes summarized by Murphy, Murphy and Newcomb, *op. cit.*, pp. 946–980.

chology of the college student" has been developed without thereby necessarily developing, in the same measure, an adequate general social psychology.

In this connection, we need note only that our informants were drawn from diverse educational levels, different religious groups, a wide range of socioeconomic strata, and varying ethnic backgrounds. Although these informants are not assumed to be a representative sample of those who heard the Smith broadcasts, their varied social position and cultural participation provide some ground for supposing that they provide a wider *range* of responses to the propaganda situation than would be evidenced by a more homogeneous group of subjects, such as that of college students. For purposes of a sociopsychological case study, this diversity of response is a decided asset inasmuch as it precludes overready generalizations which might be adequate to summarize more uniform responses. In short, this material approximates the desideratum laid down for such studies by the Murphys and Newcomb, inasmuch as it has "to do with realistic behavior of run-of-the-mine adults in a complex social situation."

6. *Sociocultural context*

In this case study, we have the distinct advantage of being compelled to consider the responses to the Smith broadcast in their larger context. For as the investigation developed it became abundantly clear that the basis of persuasion by Smith included far more than the manifest content of her radio appeals. It was a larger configuration in which the audience's images of Smith, the class structure of our society, the cultural standards of distinct strata of the population, and socially induced expectations, feelings, tensions were all intricately involved in the patterns of response to the bond drive. Nor are we refashioning this episode to conform with our own preconceptions in viewing it as mirroring some of the salient features of our culture. Quite the contrary.

The investigation proceeded initially on the assumption that it would be adequate, in a first approximation, to interpret responses to the Smith bond drive primarily on the basis of the content of her appeals. It was only when this approach proved clearly unprofitable, it was only when analysis of the actual responses showed an elaborate network of cultural symbolisms and of unquestionable reference to a wider social context, that we were compelled to enlarge our perspectives. We found that in our initial definition of the problem we were being not hardheaded but pigheaded. The process of persuasion did not consist of atomistic responses to a limited number of readily detectible stimuli. Listeners responded differently in terms of their constructions of "what Kate Smith was really like." Other responses clearly involved reference to the "kind of world in which we live."

The ways in which certain traits imputed by listeners to Smith entered into the process of persuasion could be understood only within the context of our social structure. Thus, the enormous importance ascribed to her integrity reflected our subjects' conviction, partly based on experience and magnified by consequent anxiety, that they are often the object of exploitation, manipulation and control by others who have their own private interests at heart. The emphasis on this theme reflects a social disorder—"anomie" is the sociological term—in which common values have been submerged in the welter of private interests seeking satisfaction by virtually any means which are effective. It is a product of a society in which "salesmanship"—in the sense of selling through deft pretense of concern with the other fellow—has run riot. Only against this background of skepticism and distrust stemming from a prevalently manipulative society were we able to interpret our subjects' magnified "will to believe" in a public figure who is thought to incarnate the virtues of sincerity, integrity, good-fellowship and altruism. In short, listeners brought to the Smith broadcast a wealth of wants and expectations which had been organized by the run of experience which our society had fashioned for them. This case study guides us to the social and cultural context of mass persuasion, a context which might well have been overlooked in a more rigorous laboratory experiment.

In these six respects, then, the Smith bond drive provides us with materials appropriate for a case study of mass persuasion. Our intensive analysis of this case should serve two purposes. It should enable us to ferret out from the complexities of a concrete life situation the variables which appear to be decisive in determining whether persuasion does or does not occur. And, second, it should permit us to discern the processes and dynamisms involved in such persuasion. The case study thus serves as a prelude to experimentation, by providing a realistic basis for selecting the variables to be included in experiments. It provides a bridge, so to speak, from the concreteness of everyday life to the abstractions of experimental inquiry. It is no mere metaphor to say that this case study may be construed as a clinical inquiry, designed to yield an orientation for the further experimental study of propaganda and persuasion.

The Raw Materials

It is one thing to say that we are concerned with the study of mass persuasion and another to specify in detail the character of our problem. Gross data can provide only gross, and unilluminating, results. Thus, it will be of small service to emerge from this study with a conclusion of the type recently advanced by a social psychologist: "Persuasion makes use of trigger phrases which suggest to us values we desire to realize and tells that we may realize them by means of the course of action proposed." For, although it may well be that this statement is by and large true, it affords little insight into the pertinent questions. Which trigger phrases prove persuasive and which do not? Further, which people are persuaded and which are not? And what are the processes involved in such persuasion and in resistance to persuasive arguments? In short, we can understand the social psychology of persuasion only when we analyze both the content of the propaganda and the responses of the audience to it. The analysis of the content, what is said, gives us clues to what might be effective in it. The analysis of responses to the broadcasts enables us to check these clues. Working back and forth between these two, we may obtain the answer to the chief problem: why are certain types of listeners moved to action whereas others remain unmoved? This is what we mean by *differential analysis* of content and response.

Content Analysis. One of the most decisive steps forward in recent studies of propaganda has involved the practice of specification of the effective stimulus patterns. Earlier investigations were satisfied with establishing the over-all effects of an unanalyzed propaganda document. Thus, Thurstone was able to demonstrate experimentally that an anti-Negro film— *The Birth of a Nation*—increased anti-Negro sentiments in test audiences. In similar fashion, we may discover that the "Kate Smith bond appeals effectually led to bond pledges," without materially adding to our understanding of the workings of persuasion. Such gross statements patently tell us little about the *distinctive elements or structure* of the persuasion materials which produced this result. We can hardly hope to interpret the effects of the stimulus pattern unless the stimulus pattern itself is adequately known. A prior content analysis of the Smith scripts is designed, therefore, to single out, on a hypothetical basis, those characteristics of her appeals which might be expected to elicit particular types of responses from her audience. By suggesting such clues to probable responses, the content analysis provides a partial guide for interviews with persons who heard the Smith broadcasts. The interviews in turn serve as a check on the validity of our hypotheses concerning responses to the bond appeals.[5]

The Focused Interviews. One hundred detailed interviews[6] with persons who heard the Smith bond broadcasts provided the basic materials for this pilot study. Of these, 75 were drawn from the lists of those who had telephoned their bond pledges to WABC, the New York outlet of the Columbia Broadcasting System. They were persons who had presumably been "persuaded" by Smith, at least to the extent of purchasing their bonds in response to her appeal. For comparative purposes, we interviewed 25 persons who, although they had heard the Smith broadcasts, did not respond by purchasing a bond. These "unpersuaded" listeners were located after persistent inquiry in various neighborhoods of New York City. Since our primary interest lay in discerning the processes and elements of persuasion, no effort was made to obtain a sample of informants representative of Smith's national audience on the occasion of the bond drive.

The interviews, which were conducted in the homes of subjects, were intensive, lasting some three to four hours. Interviewing began the day following the broadcast, and fully half the interviews were completed within a week. The bulk of the others were conducted during the week following. In some 65 cases, subjects were reinterviewed, in order to sup-

[5] For a brief statement of this type of procedure, see P. F. Lazarsfeld and R. K. Merton, "Studies in Radio and Film Propaganda," *Transactions of the New York Academy of Sciences*, 6 (1943), 58–79.

[6] The sex, age, economic and religious composition of this group is reported in Appendix B.

plement or confirm conjectures drawn from the initial inter-view data. Since experience had shown that informants were not disturbed by the note-taking of interviewers, a detailed circumstantial transcript of the interview was obtained in all instances. In some cases, interviewers recorded the interview stenographically.

Interviewers were trained in the special techniques of what we term the "focused interview," a type of inquiry designed to determine responses to a *particular* communication, or stimu-lus pattern, which has been previously analyzed by the inves-tigator. Interviewers seldom asked direct, predetermined questions of the informants. Instead, through appropriate indirect allusions stemming from the flow of conversation, they encouraged informants to dwell upon their concrete experi-ences, their thoughts and feelings and behavior while they had been listening to the Smith broadcasts. Thus, the interviewer's comments did not direct attention toward certain aspects of the propaganda. Informants provided their own definitions of the situation. They, not the interviewer, singled out the per-tinent aspects of the situation to which they had responded. In this sense, the interviews were largely "nondirective," permit-ting subjects to report their own foci of attention and their own responses to those items which proved significant for them.

Moreover, in place of reporting the gross segments of the broadcasts which elicited given responses, informants were encouraged to *specify* what they perceived in the Smith appeals. Only after the interviewees had reported in detail their responses to the aspects of the broadcasts which they had experienced most vividly did the interviewers round out the discussion by raising additional questions drawn from an inter-view guide[7] (based on the content analysis). To a consider-

[7] The interview guide is reproduced in Appendix A.

able degree, our materials satisfied the criteria of an effective focused interview:[8]

1. *range:* they provided extensive reports of the evocative stimulus patterns contained in the Smith appeals;
2. *specificity:* they contained specific accounts of the informants' definition of the Smith broadcasts;
3. *depth and personal context:* they revealed the emotional and value-laden contexts of responses to the appeals as well as the central or peripheral character of the experience; and
4. *nondirection:* they involved a minimum of guidance and direction by the interviewer.

In many instances, our informants revealed more than they realized. Their spontaneous allusions to the emotional contexts within which they responded to the Smith bond appeals provided clues to the symbolisms and images contained in their listening experience. There can be little question of the deep ego involvement experienced by a large proportion of our informants. In the course of some interviews, informants reinstated the anxieties, fears and sympathy which attended the initial responses to the appeals. At times, their emotional tension flowed over into tears. They spoke freely of their humiliation as they realized their own inadequate contributions to the war effort when measured by the sacrifices reported by Smith. They exhibited little resistance to describing in detail the routines of experience which culminated in their decision to pledge additional war bonds. They provided concrete, vivid reports. Just as most people are seldom conscious of the grammatical structure of what they say, so these informants did not realize they were expressing their images of Smith, their social evaluations and prejudices, their fears, anxieties and hopes.

[8] These criteria are drawn from an extensive handbook of interviewing procedures. For an abbreviated version of this handbook, see Robert K. Merton and Patricia L. Kendall, "The Focused Interview," *The American Journal of Sociology*, 51 (1946), 541-57.

In short, the atmosphere of the intensive interview permitted us to obtain vivid accounts of the flow of experience set in motion by the Smith broadcasts. These interviews, which constitute the bulk of our material, were supplemented by more extensive quantitative data.

The Polling Interviews. As our initial analysis of the focused interview materials proceeded, it became evident that some of our hypothetical interpretations could be granted credibility only if we obtained|pertinent information on a more extended statistical basis. The interviews had suggested, for example, that the responses to Smith's appeals were significantly affected by certain images of Smith current among our interviewees. Similarly, there was considerable qualitative evidence that belief in Smith's disinterestedness and altruism played an integral role in the process of persuasion. What we could not learn, on the basis of a hundred cases, was the prevalence of these images and imputed motivations among the public at large.

In order to secure information that might serve as a check on our preliminary analyses, we conducted a supplementary polling interview with 978 persons, representing a carefully selected cross section of the Greater New York population.[9] By addressing a limited number of strategic questions to this cross section, we obtained pertinent statistical data which enabled us to test certain hypotheses based on our qualitative materials. Although it was not practicable to subject all of our hypotheses to such further test, this general procedure of devising appropriate extensive interviews after preliminary analysis of intensive interviews may, in the future, serve to marry the distinctive merits of the two types of material: the one, providing a basis for processual analysis in social psy-

[9] The questions in the polling interview are reproduced in Appendix A.

chology; the other, testing the relative frequency of the patterns of responses which have been previously ascertained.

In summary, then, this study is based on three sets of interrelated data: content analysis of the Smith radio broadcasts; intensive focused interviews with a hundred persons who heard her bond broadcasts; and polling interviews, confined to certain specific questions, with a cross section of almost one thousand persons. Each set of material has its own distinctive function. The content analysis enables us to determine the "objective" characteristics of the broadcasts to which various responses occurred; the intensive interviews permit us to discover the components and processes involved in persuasion; and the extensive interviews provide a partial check of some of these interpretations.

Plan of the Study

More than sixty broadcasts by one person throughout the day may be held to constitute a radio marathon. In the next chapter, we shall look into the organization of this marathon, with an eye to its effectiveness as a device for riveting the attention of a large audience upon a single person.

The third chapter introduces a thematic analysis of the war bond appeals. In it, we examine the content of what was said, what was sedulously avoided, and how listeners responded to the themes running through the Smith broadcasts.

Chapter 4 analyzes the images of public figures and idols and the compatibility of these with the emotional meanings of war bonds. The images prevalently held of Smith are related to her effectiveness as a purveyor of patriotism for certain audiences.

With the knowledge gained from hindsight, we examine in Chapter 5 the prevailing attitudes of our subjects toward the purchase of war bonds and relate these predispositions to the likelihood of persuasion by Smith. The varying effects of the Smith drive upon listeners in different states of mind are explored in detail.

In Chapter 6, we consider the social and cultural context of Smith's techniques of persuasion. How does a radio singer come to gain a following in spheres far removed from mass entertainment? What does this imply about the society in which prestige can diffuse in this fashion?

A brief concluding chapter sums up our findings and the light which they cast on the moral dilemma presented by strategies of mass persuasion.

Throughout the emphasis is placed on the interrelations of these several elements. For just as the effectiveness of Smith's war bond drive cannot be explained if her appeals are considered in isolation, apart from the prevailing social images of the person who made these appeals, so the entire event—the war bond drive—cannot be adequately interpreted if it is severed from the cultural context in which it occurred. The several components of the war bond drive—the social imagery of Smith, her appeals, the marathon structure of the drive, the predispositions of listeners, the social setting in which Smith exhibits her characteristic personality traits—these components are woven deep into a social and cultural contexture, and it is our aim to keep this unfailingly in mind. Yet, in our exposition, we cannot consider these various elements simultaneously; they must be examined in sequence. It is for the reader, as well as the writer, to recognize the essential interdependence of the several factors comprised by the war bond drive, even when they are examined serially rather than in conjuncture. The marathon structure provides the framework for the several appeals; the appeals operate as they do partly because of the public personality of the person who sets them forth; the reactions to this personality are inextricably bound up with certain features of the American culture; and all of these—marathon, appeals, public personality, and culture—articulate into a single whole: the Smith war bond drive of September 21, 1943.

Rhetorick, that Faculty, by which we understand what will serve our turn, concerning any Subject to win belief in the hearer.

Of those things that beget belief; some require not the help of Art; as *Witnesses, Evidences*, and the like, which we invent not, but make use of; and some require Art, and are invented by us.

The belief that proceeds from our Invention, comes partly from the *behaviour* of the speaker; partly from the *passions* of the *hearer:* but especially from the *proofs* of what we alledge.

Proofs are, in *Rhetorick*, either *Examples*, or *Enthymemes*, as in *Logick, Inductions*, or *Syllogisms*. For an *Example* is a short *Induction*, and an *Enthymeme* a short *Syllogisme;* out of which are left as superfluous, that which is supposed to be necessarily understood by the hearer; to avoid prolixity, and not to consume the time of the publick business needlessly.

* * * *

For as in *Logick*, where certain and infallible knowledg is the scope of our proof; the *Principles* must be all *infallible truths:* so in *Rhetorick* the *Principles* must be *common opinions*, such as the Judg is already possessed with: because the end of *Rhetorick* is victory; which consists in having gotten *belief.*

* * * *

Forasmuch as there is nothing more delightful to a Man, than to find that he apprehends and learns easily; it necessarily follows, that those *Words* are most *grateful* to the Ear, that make a man seem to see before his Eyes the things signified.

—Tho. Hobbes, of Malmsbury, *The Art of Rhetorick plainly set forth; with pertinent Examples for the more easie understanding and Practice of the same* (London: W. Crook, 1681)

Chapter 2

THE MARATHON: A TEMPORAL PATTERN

AN APPEAL broadcast nation-wide every quarter hour throughout the day creates a distinctive kind of social and psychological situation. Of course, the sheer recurrence of appeals increases the likelihood that any given radio listener will hear some of them, but the differences between such a daylong drive and the usual series of discrete programs are more than quantitative. When a single, widely known person speaks so often and at such short intervals, the listener's experience takes on new qualities. That is to say, hearing Smith ten times in an evening does not produce a psychological response which is merely ten distinct reactions to a single program. On the contrary, it constitutes a new and different type of experience. The event emerges as distinctive against the background of more usual radio programs. In the language of Gestalt psychology, it stands out like a figure against the ground. The repeated pleas merge into a cumulative whole and the series seems to move toward some climax. The successive appeals form a pattern, and this psychological structure, which might be described as a time-bound configuration, is felt by the listener to be different from an aggregate of separate stimuli. The speaker becomes not just a casual announcer reading a prepared script as part of a bread-and-butter job, but a central actor in a moving drama, a drama in which the listener himself plays a part.

We shall first explore some of these general aspects of this type of radio marathon—*aspects independent of the particular theme and speaker.* Anyone broadcasting repeatedly as did Smith would have certain great advantages in achieving mass persuasion. It is our purpose to analyze these aspects before going on to the special characteristics introduced because of Smith's social personality and her public role.

An Outstanding Event

From the time of the first war bond campaign, Americans have been exposed to radio appeals asking them to buy a bond. Celebrities and nonentities, persons with and without prestige, have presented messages, for the most part in stereotyped form. The pattern of appeals, replete with standardized phrases, had become a routine toward which some members of the radio audience had become indifferent or hostile. Against this routine background, the all-day series of appeals emerged as a dramatic occasion. Only two of the hundred listeners interviewed failed to characterize the Smith bond drive as distinctive, isolating it from an otherwise homogeneous environment of bond appeals on the air.

When the day's broadcasts began, Smith explained that this was no ordinary event.

"I'm going to appear on CBS programs *throughout the day* from now until one o'clock tomorrow morning."

"I've been in radio quite some time, folks, but in all those years *I don't think anything even remotely like this has ever been done before.*"

This was hyperbole. There had been other radio broadcasters who had made repeated pleas during a day, which resembled more than remotely the Smith marathon. But these instances were few and had not been so widely publicized.

The contours of a striking and unusual event were further defined by Smith's account of what all this would mean to her:

> "This is Kate Smith again, working on what I hope and believe is going to be *the most wonderful . . . the proudest . . . day of my whole life.*"

And not only Smith, but the whole vast mysterious machinery of a radio network must be recognized as animated by this extraordinary occasion.

> "This is CBS Bond Day. It's the day when we—and when I say we, I mean all of us here at CBS and all of its stations all over the network—are getting together to make a dream come true."

The success of the enterprise led to further disruption of usual routines.

> "*All regular business at this station has been suspended, with the entire staff manning the telephones.*"

Thus the special character of these broadcasts was underscored for the most casual listener. Every hour of the day and in about every third broadcast, Smith referred to the daylong nature of her program.

> "I'll be on the air *all day* today . . ."

> "In the studio where I am now and where I'm going to be *all day* . . ."

> "I'm working *all day long* . . ."

Commentators on other CBS programs wove their comments into the fabric of expectation. There was little possibility of escaping the atmosphere of excited anticipation. As one listener reported the mounting tension, "I was getting more and more excited. Calls were coming in and she wanted to push things through. She was getting more and more excited and I liked her better and better all the time."

Toward the end of the marathon the references increasingly emphasized Smith's long and arduous effort, producing a psychological effect of great importance which we shall analyze in a later chapter, but also making it clear to latecomers that the broadcast they heard was part of an out-of-the-ordinary performance.

Listeners clearly felt that they were witnessing or even participating in a special event. Some recognized the parallel structure of Smith's drive and other types of marathons:

> "I heard announcers saying, 'Back to Kate Smith who is on her 14th hour.' *It was attention-getting,* more than saying, for example, 'Carole Landis is going to make an appeal.' We're used to hearing reports like this. In the 20's we used to hear about marathon dancers, air records, flagpole sitters, nurses who put in so many hours, etc."

In a variety of respects, then, the Smith sequence of appeals was so structured as to focus the attention of the audience on its special attributes. In this fashion, the designers of the bond drive virtually followed the precept of a student of public opinion who observed: "The art of persuasion consists largely in directing attention to those aspects of a subject that will influence the mind of the person to be persuaded."[1] And, as we shall see, the implications of the marathon played no small role in predisposing listeners to persuasion by Smith.

The Marathon Gestalt and Compulsive Listening

For most of our informants the marathon had taken on the character of a single unified pattern. Spot announcements at odd moments during the radio day are usually discrete. Each

[1] A. L. Lowell, *Public Opinion in War and Peace* (Cambridge: Harvard University Press, 1926), p. 26.

is complete in itself. Listeners who hear several such announcements do not respond to them as a series or unity. In contrast, the Smith war bond drive was experienced by most informants not as a procession of unrelated parts, but as an integral event enduring all day and into the night. The early announcements foreshadowed later reports. Later comments reported audience reactions to earlier broadcasts. The marathon had a beginning in the morning and an end eighteen hours later. The Gestalt, or configurative quality, was so marked that it bridged over the longer interludes of music, news and other programs. Just as an arrangement of dots in space can convey the outline of a triangle, the brief intervals of Smith's broadcasts were linked across time into the pattern of one continuing event:

> "It was not just a bond rally by fifty Hollywood stars or a thousand people gathered together on Fifth Avenue, but just one person was managing the whole thing. I suppose it was the length of time she was on the air that gave *the focus of a single person.*"

One immediate consequence of this time-binding structure was a frequent compulsion to continue listening. Fully half of the hundred informants had listened to Smith more than ten times that day. Thirty-two per cent had heard her from eleven to forty times, and 16 per cent on more than forty occasions during the one day of the drive.[2]

But these high proportions do not fully reflect the degree of continued listening. Some of those who first heard the Smith broadcasts in the morning could not continue to listen if only because they had to leave the house to carry on their normal routines. And a considerable proportion of those who had

[2] These figures are not based merely on estimates by informants, which would inevitably have a large margin of error. Such estimates were checked by three types of information: (1) the hours of continuous listening to WABC on that day reported by informants; (2) the extent to which listeners attended to the Smith broadcasts; (3) the actual frequency of Smith's broadcasts during these intervals.

heard her fewer than ten times failed to hear more broadcasts
only because they began their listening late in the day, and so
had little opportunity to prolong it. Of those who tuned in
before noon and thus had this opportunity, 70 per cent listened
more than ten times; 59 per cent more than twenty times and
26 per cent more than forty times.[3] This indicates sustained
interest to an extraordinary degree.

It appears, moreover, that this continuous listening was not
merely a by-product of listening to the usual routine of radio
programs on the Columbia Broadcasting System and thus inadvertently hearing Smith's periodic appeals. It was not only
continued, but more nearly compulsive, listening. In order to
follow the sequence of the marathon, 54 per cent of the informants fixed their attention on the radio program considerably more than usual. The listening practices of 38 per cent
were not appreciably affected by the marathon and only 5 per
cent reduced their listening to CBS programs in order to escape
Smith's insistent entreaties.

The internal consistency of two sets of data—amount of
listening and number of Smith broadcasts heard—confirm these
judgments by informants. The proportion of informants reporting that they "listened more than usual" increases as the
number of Smith broadcasts heard increases. Thus, although

[3] The relationship between the time of initial listening and the number
of Smith broadcasts heard are summarized in the following tabulation:

No. of Smith Broadcasts Heard	Time of Initial Listening			
	Before Noon	Between Noon and 6 p.m.	After 6 p.m.	Total
	%	%	%	%
1–10	30	78	93	50
11–20	11	22	7	13
21–40	33	—	—	21
41–over	26	—	—	16
Total per cent	100	100	100	100
No. of cases	(63)	(23)	(14)	(100)

only a third of those who heard Smith ten times or less report having "listened more than usual," all eighteen of those who heard her on more than forty occasions report a rise in radio listening.[4]

Finally, the testimony of informants shows clearly that this increase in radio listening took on a virtually compulsive character.

"*We never left her that day. We stood by her side.* I didn't go out all day, except to go shopping. *Even then, I was anxious to get back and listen. Of course, my sister was holding down the post in the meantime and could tell me what had happened.*"

The compulsive element in continued listening becomes obvious when informants speak of actually having wanted to escape Smith's insistent demands, but of being "unable" to do so.

"I was glad at the end of the day when her job was over and *I didn't have to listen to her any more.*"

In extreme cases, attention was so fixed on the continuance of an ongoing event that it actually obscured avenues for escape from a painful experience. Listeners did not consider the alternatives of turning off the radio, tuning in another program, or merely failing to listen closely. The solution to their problem

[4] This corroborative evidence is summarized in the following table:

Amount of Listening	Number of Smith Broadcasts Heard			
	1–10	11–20	21 and over	Total
	%	%	%	%
More than usual	33	69	81	55
Same as usual	58	31	19	40
Less than usual	9	—	—	5
Total	100	100	100	100
Cases	(48)	(13)	(36)	(97)
No answer	(2)	—	(1)	(3)
Total interviewed	(50)	(13)	(37)	(100)

waited in a vestibule of consciousness, but was not admitted to awareness as a result of focusing their attention on Smith's continuing broadcasts.

> "It was actually hounding you to get a bond. *Possibly if the radio wasn't on all day I would have let it go.*"

> "Usually I get tired of listening and I turn it off. It's funny, whenever there is any commercial on, you turn it off, but then I had it on all afternoon. *I didn't realize it at the time, but I had to keep listening.*"

All this suggests that the tyranny of radio proved altogether compelling. And it raises several distinct questions. Why permit oneself to be "hounded" by a radio broadcast? Why not escape by a twist of the dials? Since this phenomenon of compulsive listening was integral to the process of persuasion, it calls for detailed study.

Approach Toward a Goal

Almost everyone has had the experience of being interrupted in the pursuit of some goal on which he had set his mind, and can recall how uneasy he felt until he could return to it. As various psychologists[5] have demonstrated by careful and ingenious experimentation, tension persists until the goal-directed activity is complete, and there is an emotional resistance to any suggestion of halting before the end is reached. This is the pattern that underlay the compulsion to which various informants testified. They were striving and straining toward a goal, particularly those who identified themselves with Smith, and there was aroused in them a psychological tension for "closure." They had to go on listening or there would be unre-

[5] See, for example, Kurt Lewin, *Vorsatz, Wille und Bedürfnis* (Berlin, Springer, 1926); M. Ovsiankina, "Die Wiederaufnahme unterbrochener Handlungen," *Psychol. Forsch.*, XI (1928), 302–379; A. R. Pachauri, "A Study of Gestalt Problems in Completed and Interrupted Tasks," *British Journal of Psychology*, 25 (1935), 365–381; 447–457.

lieved tension, a sense of incompletion. This persistence pattern helps explain why one listener left her sister at the radio to keep in touch with developments while she was away: she was responding to the series of appeals as an integral, ongoing activity that had yet to be completed.

Thus we may say that the Smith marathon was not only a totality, or Gestalt, but one of a particular type. Its structure was that of a race or an endurance contest, and it was directed toward a goal. Hence the aptness of the term "marathon."

Responding to this attribute of the drive, listeners were variously concerned with the extent of Smith's endurance. We must distinguish between two types of perseverative listeners: those who interpreted the long day's broadcast as a kind of heroic martyrdom and those for whom it was little more than a diverting race. The former, naturally, were persons who regarded the marathon as an example of Smith's readiness to sacrifice herself for a cause imbued with pathos, and we shall have much more to say about them in Chapter 4. The point to be made here is that listeners who had no such strong feelings about Smith nevertheless responded to the excitement of the marathon. For such listeners, obviously, Smith's failure to reach her goal would provide as satisfactory a release of tension as her success, and their interest derived from the possibility of failure:

> "I wanted to know how she's holding out. Is she living up to my picture of her? Will she last as long as any person could? Is she still the same robust person who never feels the pressure of her work; one who eats heartily and has a zest for life? Is she selling enough bonds to compensate? What does she sound like at this hour of the morning?"

Those few listeners who did not realize that it was a marathon preserved a detached attitude toward the day's performance. Believing that the messages were transcribed and therefore involved no "sacrifice" on Smith's part, these listeners were no more moved by the periodic appeals than by other spot announcements. A listener who only the next morning learned from a newspaper story that Smith had indeed spoken in person throughout the day explained her lack of interest in the drive: "At the time I heard it, I thought it was a recording. I didn't think that a woman would sit in a radio station all day like that."

A secular group atmosphere also facilitated this detached attitude of a spectator, as may be seen in the following case. A male informant reported the spirit of a group listening in a saloon which was that of a crowd watching a weight lifter, a toreador, or a tightrope walker:

> "After each announcement *there was a sort of tension in the place to see whether she would come on again.* There were two other fellows at the other end of the bar when we first came in. After a while, they wanted to lay odds that she wouldn't stay on till two o'clock. There were 35 men in the place and one woman. I left at one, I don't know what happened, but I think many of them stayed because *they wanted to see what would be the outcome of her endurance.*"

> "One fellow wanted to have the radio turned off. Well, the reaction was that he was going to be thrown out. Nobody wanted it turned off."

> "Every time she spoke we discussed whether she had been stronger or weaker than in the last 15 minutes and *just when it would be safe to bet on her ending.* We at this end of the bar were of the opinion that she would go off at midnight. The manager said that if she went off then he would buy the house a drink. Well, we didn't get that drink, and I think a lot of the fellows were disappointed."

Tension was maintained until Smith's final broadcast was heard at two in the morning. In this case, and in that of the woman who said, "I took it for granted she would hold out; I didn't think she'd undertake it if she couldn't hold out," the attitude is clearly that of an observer who is not himself very much identified with Smith. Sometimes, however, informants provide evidence of a dual role as spectator and as sympathetic vicarious participant, in which anxiety about Smith's endurance led to perseverative listening:

"She just thrilled me because she was so full of pep and so warmhearted. *I prayed that her voice would hold out.*"

There is at least a hint of suspicion that perhaps the voice would break.

The idea that her voice and energy might not endure was suggested by Smith herself several times early in the day, and as the evening wore on she contributed something to the continued excitement and anxiety by a voice that sounded fatigued. One listener who admired Smith especially because of the "power that keeps her going," noted in the evening, "The voice gave out. It was getting weaker. Her finish was, 'Will you buy a bond?' and it was weaker and weaker."

The performer who is on the verge of failure evokes sustained interest. No one is much interested in seeing a weight lifter toss up ten pounds; there is no zest in watching him fail to budge a thousand pounds, but somewhere in between, where he might succeed or might fail, the spectators hold their breath. It is comparable to the appeal of the tightwire act which is well reflected in the story of the man who followed the circus from one town to another. His friends assumed he was in love with the girl acrobat, only to have him explain: "I just want to be sure I'm there when she finally slips and falls." Between the region of the easily possible and the region of the clearly impossible lies the region of challenge. One effective aspect of Smith's drive, serving to focus the interest of the audience, was the introduction of this hint that perhaps she had taken on more than she could do, leading the vicarious participant to continue his listening to discover whether Smith's capacity would measure up to her aspiration.[6]

Those who identified themselves closely with Smith found themselves very much concerned with her physical condition, and rooting for her to succeed. Often, Smith was pictured virtually approaching collapse as she moved toward the close of her campaign:

> "I think she went on at 6 a.m. Later her voice cracked. I remember her doing the same thing in the last drive, so I didn't think she'd crack. I felt that if her voice should hesitate entirely, *I hoped that a lot of people would rush in and revive her with the response of buying bonds.*"

An empathic listener waited until midnight to buy because she thought an impetus in sales at that late hour might give Smith a needed fillip.

> "*I thought it would sort of help then.* It's like myself. When I'm tired, a cup of coffee will do a lot for me."

Inherent in the projection of a goal was the listener's responsibility for helping to attain that goal, and avert failure. Yet the idea of a goal was not utilized in the broadcasts as fully as it might have been. Anyone who has watched election returns or a financial drive for a given quota will recall the excitement of the closing hours. The thermometer readings climb nearer and nearer the goal and the tension of the audience rises with it. Had the bond drive set an objective within the region of challenge—not too easy and not impossible—then the dynamic effect of the established goal would have been more pronounced. Smith spoke of making her dream come true, but it was not clear how high the figures of her dream might run.

[6] Studies of the level of aspiration have found that perseveration continues when the task is neither too far above nor too far below the level of aspiration. See F. Hoppe, "Erfolg und Misserfolg," *Psychol. Forsch.*, 14 (1930), 1–62; Rosalind Gould, "An Experimental Analysis of Levels of Aspiration," *Genetic Psychology Monographs*, 21 (1939), 1–116.

She did speak at one time of every man, woman and child in the United States buying a bond, a goal so clearly beyond the practical that it lacked full psychological potency.

Nevertheless, the sense of an approaching climax did develop during the evening.

> "By then I was gripped by some sort of competitive racing spirit, intent on seeing how figures climb, much as one would when following election returns over the radio."

Another listener supplied the crowning factor herself, incidentally testifying to the integral character of the day's drive. She listened from eight in the morning until noon and again from five in the afternoon until past midnight. "I wanted to be the last sale," she said. Thus she could bring the whole day to a fitting culmination. She could personally effect consummation of the drive.

Repetition

The marathon structure also provided opportunity for effective persuasion through continued repetition. At the close of each broadcast, Smith repeated the slogan "Will you buy a bond?" a phrase mentioned more often by listeners than any other specific content of her broadcasts. It proved to be a cue for the entire series of more complex experiences less easily recalled and served to reinstate them:

> "She told some wonderful stories. She was going through a terrible strain all day. She was pleading, 'Will you *please* buy a bond?' [This said with the Smith inflection] *I can still hear her.*"

The slogan served to crystallize and epitomize the feelings and tensions involved in the situation.[7] "It was her effective

---

[7] Cf. Muzafer Sherif, "The Psychology of Slogans," *Journal of Abnormal and Social Psychology*, 32 (1937), 450–461. Significantly enough, informants repeatedly called to mind another slogan utilized in the weekly Smith program: "I like the way she gives you a hint—'If you don't write, you're wrong' —to sort of tell you to write to the boys."

ending, 'Will you buy a bond?' The way she asked it, you just had to."

Others refer to the cumulative impact of Smith's successive appeals. As each link in the chain of broadcasts was rounded out, listeners anticipated the next. The one unvarying phrase helped provide a sense of continuity, despite intervening radio programs:

> "Every time she closed 'Will you buy a bond?' And each time she surprised me because she didn't do it monotonously or melodramatically. I *found myself listening for the phrase after each broadcast*, and the variety with which Kate was able to say those words was more impressive than the stories. It seemed to get more impressive each time."

The potency of repetition in persuading others to act has been widely recognized but not often analyzed. Hitler is authority, howsoever dubious, for the observation that even a great lie will be believed if it is asserted often enough. Experienced advertisers do not expect results from a slogan until it has been frequently repeated. The child seems aware that his mother who says "No" at first may relent if he teases long enough. But why does a stimulus applied successive times have an effect the nth time which it did not have the first? We resort to such analogies as that of the drip of water wearing away a stone, recognizing that they do not adequately illuminate the complex psychological processes of persuasion through repetition. Many of our listeners were aware of the effect and tried variously to characterize it. "She got you," said one informant, groping for words to express the effect of the same voice coming at her again and again, every quarter hour. "I couldn't stand it any longer," said another. But why attempt to stand it? And why did it prove so difficult to withstand?

It is widely recognized that simple repetition is not always effective. Very often it induces boredom, surfeit or active irritation,[8] or at least a kind of defensive isolation. Thus people who live with the constant ticking of a noisy clock, the crowing of roosters, the rumble of a noisy furnace, or even the roar of passing trains, become so accommodated to these sounds that they pay no attention to them. What develops in such instances is a repeated pattern of ignoring the stimulus, and this pattern can be observed in the reaction of some radio listeners to the flow of routine appeals to buy bonds. The multiplication of spot announcements, instead of stimulating purchases, may lead to satiety and "radio deafness."

What is it, then, that determines whether repetition results in surfeit or in enhanced interest? If Smith's marathon did not induce boredom, this was because it was largely experienced as a single, continuing event rather than as a collection of unchanging, repeated appeals. Listeners who had grown deaf to routine pleas responded enthusiastically to the marathon appeal and purchased bonds from Smith.[9] The same shopkeeper who used funds set aside for her grandchild's layette in order to buy a bond from Smith spoke of her indifference to the ordinary flow of incessant appeals over the air:

" . . . every program is buy bonds . . . The stories you hear every day, the whole day long, about buying bonds. *You don't even listen.*"

So, too, with another informant who had developed a definite hostility toward the bond campaign:

---

[8] Note Bartlett's observation: "If news and views are communicated which can be very easily assimilated, parrot-like repetition soon tends to produce boredom . . . If the communication has to meet definite opposition, already formed in the listeners, sheer repetition soon stirs anger or contempt . . ." F. C. Bartlett, *Political Propaganda* (Cambridge: The University Press, 1940), p. 69.

[9] It was not merely the structure of the marathon that led to the Smith bond drive being distinguished from the usual run of appeals and, accordingly, to differences in listener response. Other factors which led to Smith being prevailingly singled out as a "figure" against the competing "ground" will be considered in Chapter 4.

"I'm already saturated with all the other appeals to buy . . ."

Smith's continued appeals did not typically arouse these defensive mechanisms for yet another reason. The reports by informants and an analysis of Smith's broadcasts both indicate that *the marathon did not consist of simple repetitions.* The marathon utilized the classic formula of diversity within unity.

> "She kept telling stories; they were all vivid and very touching. It was different each time."

> "What struck me . . . was the way she kept saying, 'Won't you please buy a bond?' The sort of tormenting way in which she did it, and she told little incidents of how people were suffering in Europe. She did a very good job—so good that she made me hock my wedding ring."

The "Will you buy a bond?" slogan may have served as an easily remembered theme, but each appeal contained a new instance, a new perspective, or struck a new note.

Repetition with variation of appeals proved an important element in the process of persuasion.[10] Smith's broadcasts aimed at one and the same goal, but each was unique. The effect, therefore, was not one of mere reiteration. And the goal, in this instance, was an act which the listener was expected to perform. Each new entreaty sought out a new *vulnerability* in some listeners.

> "What got me was she never repeated herself. Each time she said something that broke your heart a little more."

[10] ". . . it is not sheer repetition that is influential, but repetition with variations. What is wanted is something to break down the opposition. So far as propaganda is concerned, the requirement is to repeat with variations each time in the accompanying comment or circumstances, and each time so to shape the accompaniments that some new welcoming tendency stands a chance of being brought into play. So, gradually, the piling up of tendencies favorable to acceptance overcomes the opposition, while yet, a certain quality of opposition being still present, the communication does not lose all interest and become a bore." Bartlett, *op. cit.*, pp. 69–70. In the present instance, continued interest and listening appeared to be less a product of such "opposition" than of the tension-sustaining structure of the marathon.

Continuous listening to such varied appeals enhanced the likelihood of persuasion. A listener might ward off one attack, but a few minutes later another approach might find the weak chink in his spiritual armor. He would be persuaded not because of the identity or number of thrusts to be parried but because one of the varied thrusts at last reached his Achilles heel. In some cases, especially among those who had considered their bond-buying obligations discharged, there is evidence that a cumulation of diverse appeals proved decisive:

> "*It built you up as she went along.* Each time she came on, she had a different little incident or story. It made you feel you want to do something."

> "I didn't decide right away. I'd bought four bonds on Monday and wasn't planning to buy another. But around noontime, I decided. *As it went along, I felt she was bringing out the right points.*"

Such flexible repetition proved especially effective in bearing down on the conscience of those listeners who had not met their self-imposed quota of bond purchases. The spontaneous reports offered by our informants are not conclusive evidence, but do suggest the process involved. Smith's culturally unimpeachable demands were couched in such terms as to lead listeners to assess their own bond-buying behavior. When she asked "Will you buy a bond?" the question was utilized as a basis for self-judgment: "Should I not be buying that bond?" Each external appeal was reinforced for them by internal sense of guilt.

> "I felt that I can't stand this any longer. If I hadn't bought, I'd have felt just like dying."

What became intolerable for many was the continuous self-appraisal induced by Smith's appeals and the resulting dissatisfaction with their own inadequacies in terms of socially established standards. New standards of comparison were introduced with each new evidence of how much others were giving, and at the close came the relentless query, "Will you buy a bond?" Only those with especially strong ego defenses could withstand the self-impeachment.

One listener waited until one in the morning, but finally Smith's persistence raised her guilt feelings above the level of tolerance. "I might as well buy it now, I thought, or I won't be able to sleep." Another believed she might be able to escape in sleep, but her husband had no such illusions:

> "I heard her about 20, 25, 30 times; at 9:15 at night I bought the bond. *She was getting you so on it, I couldn't stand it no more.* My husband said to me, 'You're not going to go to bed until you get on that damn phone and give the bond in.' "

Given a minimum of receptivity, one appeal or ten may not be enough to reinforce the latent feeling of guilt to the point where it must be relieved by an act—in this case, a bond purchase. But when listeners can be continuously exposed to a variety of invidious self-judgments over a period of time, the likelihood of inducing the desired action is considerably increased. (We shall consider the role of guilt feelings in greater detail in Chapter 5.)

Persuasion: Two-Way Communication

As a consequence of its marathon structure, Smith's drive was an essay in persuasion, rather than propaganda. Though both seek to influence action, beliefs and attitude, persuasion differs from propaganda in two technical respects.[11] It involves a higher degree of social interaction between the "persuader" and the "persuadee" and it permits the persuader to adapt his argumentation to the flow of reactions of the persons he is

[11] Compare Leonard W. Doob, *Propaganda: Its Psychology and Technique* (New York: Holt, 1935), pp. 146–149.

seeking to influence. The marathon enabled Smith to achieve a degree of *social interaction* and *flexibility of appeals* approximating that possible in face-to-face discussion, in a fashion ordinarily impossible for such an impersonal, mass medium of communication as the radio. To be sure, some radio programs achieve the appearance of direct social interaction by replying to letters which have been received in the course of a week, but such delayed responses of the broadcaster to the audience lack the comparatively direct give-and-take which the marathon made possible.

The usual run of separate and distinct appeals permits the radio audience only to *react* to the speaker and his message. During the marathon, however, there was *reciprocal interplay*, for the audience was not only responding to Smith, but she was also responding to her audience and modifying her subsequent comments as a result. Many of her broadcasts during the day were based on information supplied by listeners who telephoned details about the circumstances of their bond-buying. Thus the usual radio monologue became something of a conversation. The essence of a two-way conversation is that what each says is modified by what the other has just said or by what one anticipates the other will say in return.[12] Most radio speakers cannot take the immediate reactions of listeners into account: the marathon permitted Smith to achieve the appearance, and in part the reality, of a conversation.

As Smith referred to bond orders that had just come in, more people telephoned, half hoping that their message might win a comment from her. A widow with two sons in the army said half-apologetically:

"Of course this isn't important and I would have called anyway, and as a matter of fact I didn't know she would do it,

[12] George H. Mead, *Mind, Self and Society* (Chicago: University of Chicago Press, 1934).

but when I got back from the phone I did hear her say that she had just received a call from a widow with two sons in the service."

The interplay between Smith and her audience undoubtedly reinforced the sense of a personalized appeal and, reciprocally, the personal character of her messages helped further the sense of a conversational relationship. Thus, when Smith made such remarks as "I know you are getting tired of hearing me" she established a more intimate and personal relation to listeners. Many reported what they had said to themselves as they listened. They were talking to her in fantasy, as in the case of a woman who said after one of Smith's accounts of her daylong drive, "Here's where Katy's going to be sick tomorrow."

Even in the absence of direct connection between the act of the respondent and what Smith said when next she came on the air, it was not difficult for some listeners to imagine that she was directing her remarks or her songs to them personally, as a gesture of appreciation. This is illustrated in the case of a young woman who, having recently bought a bond, initially had no intention of purchasing another. She listened to the appeals and her conviction grew that perhaps after all she could match the "sacrifice" of others.

> "It was very dramatic, really. I came down the back stairs so that I wouldn't wake the family. It took a long time to get an answer from the station, and I felt a little odd doing something like this for the first time. But then I went back upstairs and there was Kate Smith singing 'God Bless America,' and it was marvelous."

The song was taken as a personal reward for the additional sacrifice, a result which only the recurrent pattern of the marathon could make possible.

One of a Series of Marathons

An interesting problem is raised by the fact that Smith had at the time of this study undertaken three all-day bond drives. As the broadcasts of one day tend to be structured into a whole, with a beginning and an end, so her several marathons began to take form as a series with definite characteristics. Kate Smith's drive was on the way toward becoming institutionalized within the system of bond campaigns. This meant that there must be a climax not only in her single day's drive, but also within her series of drives. Each new one must reach a greater height than any which had gone before, if her drive was to be deemed "successful." She could not maintain her status by repeating her previous level of bond pledges.

As a consequence of the series of marathons, some of Smith's most devoted listeners gave precedence to her demands upon them, over the demands of the bond drive itself. Smith preempted the spotlight and diverted attention from the presumed object of her drive. This *displacement of motives* is clearly shown in reports such as the following:

> "I was very disappointed when I heard the Gracie Allen program that evening. Gracie announced that her sponsor, an insurance company, was going to buy six million dollars worth of bonds. *They should have bought from Kate Smith. It was her day!*"

It also became clear that, basing their plans on her past behavior, some listeners had waited for Smith's drive before making a purchase which they were planning in any case.

> "We've been hearing the programs on the radio, but we're particularly fond of Kate's program *so we waited for her.* We planned to buy sometime during the week."

Some were already counting on Smith's next appearance, and were saving for it. The aftermath of one drive provided motivation for taking part in the next, thus producing a cumulative effect.

> "Boy, was I sorry I couldn't buy a bond; I just couldn't afford it. *But wait until the next drive.*"

> "Kate Smith made me feel like an awful heel that I had not done more. *This time, I mean it, nothing is going to stop me from buying a bond.* I really need a dress and had sort of planned on getting it, but what the heck—I'm not walking around in the nude yet."

If the practice of waiting for a "Kate Smith Day" or that of any other celebrity had become widespread, it would have facilitated securing an ever-increasing amount of bond pledges on that occasion at the cost of reducing the amount of bond purchases in the intervening period. To the extent that this occurred, the Smith bond sales involved a mere reallocation rather than an increase in the total amount of purchases.

Smith and the Marathon

Except for this last factor, the several features of the marathon itself would operate, presumably, regardless of who the central figure might be. Anyone who spoke one minute out of every quarter hour from early morning to late at night might profit from extensive coverage, from the focal quality of an outstanding event, from compulsive listening, from the cumulative impact of a wide variety of flexible appeals built around a main theme and repeated slogans, from the possibility of making a single Gestalt out of the day's performance, from interest in an exciting finish, and from the opportunity for interaction with the audience.

Yet no one of the persons interviewed mentioned the possibility that someone else might engage in a similar program. Was this merely because Smith had been the only one in their experience who had broadcast over a period of so many hours?

Or was it rather that there was something in the marathon which made it peculiarly appropriate for Smith? In a later discussion (Chapter 4) we shall explore what Smith's imagined personality meant to her audience, and we shall see that the marathon was considered a particularly fitting vehicle for her. But first we shall want to look at the appeals used and the actual effect of the drive in stimulating purchases.

Socrates. Then let me raise another question; there is such a thing as 'having learned'?

Gorgias. Yes.

Soc. And there is also 'having believed'?

Gor. Yes.

Soc. And is the 'having learned' the same as 'having believed,' and are learning and belief the same things?

Gor. In my judgment, Socrates, they are not the same.

Soc. And your judgment is right, as you may ascertain in this way:—If a person were to say to you, 'Is there, Gorgias, a false belief as well as a true?'—you would reply, if I am not mistaken, that there is.

Gor. Yes.

Soc. Well, but is there a false knowledge as well as a true?

Gor. No.

Soc. No, indeed; and this again proves that knowledge and belief differ.

Gor. Very true.

Soc. And yet those who have learned as well as those who have believed are persuaded?

Gor. Just so.

Soc. Shall we then assume two sorts of persuasion,—one which is the source of belief without knowledge, as the other is of knowledge?

Gor. By all means.

Soc. And which sort of persuasion does rhetoric create in courts of law and other assemblies about the just and unjust, the sort of persuasion which gives belief without knowledge, or that which gives knowledge?

Gor. Clearly, Socrates, that which only gives belief.

Soc. Then rhetoric, as would appear, is the artificer of a persuasion which creates belief about the just and unjust, but gives no instruction about them?

Gor. True.

Soc. And the rhetorician does not instruct the courts of law or other assemblies about things just and unjust, but he creates belief about them; for no one can be supposed to instruct such a vast multitude about such high matters in a short time?

—Plato, *Gorgias,* 454, 455

Chapter 3

THE BOND APPEALS: A THEMATIC ANALYSIS

Bonds: Secular or Sacred?

OF THE wide range of appeals that might have been utilized to persuade Americans to buy war bonds, the Smith drive selected a battery especially suited to her public personality and her audience. Analyzing her broadcasts, one is immediately struck by two omissions. In the first place, *nothing* was said about bonds as a *sound investment*, a nest egg of security, or a promise of good things to be bought after the war. In general, bond campaigns have tried to appeal to both patriotism and economic self-interest. Nine per cent of radio spot announcements in one national campaign, for example, dwelt upon the theme of "future security." But this was evidently felt to be too materialistic and mercenary a view, and one out of accord with the dedicated spirit in which a Smith audience would buy bonds. By omitting this argument, the authors of her scripts were able to avoid the strain and incompatibility between the two main lines of motivation: unselfish, sacrificing love of country and economic motives of sound investment. The conflict between the "sacred" area of patriotism and the "profane" area of private gain[1] occurs repeatedly, as informants make abundantly clear:

[1] Deriving his conceptions from Emile Durkheim, at least one social psychologist has clearly expressed this conflict: "Now, the worlds of ordinary and Nationalistic things are different and incompatible. In the first, we seek our own welfare, in the second we sacrifice it. These two kinds of life are almost mutually exclusive. We cannot give ourselves to the ideal being (the fatherland) to whom the cult is addressed, and to ourselves and our own

"We don't buy bonds as an *investment*."

"I don't think it's *patriotic* to buy bonds. What's patriotic in saving money and getting more for it? *It's my duty*. They're asking for little and giving us more in return. The boys are doing the noble work. We're just giving a few lousy dollars, if you'll excuse me."

Smith helped to resolve the conflict by greatly strengthening *one* of the two appeals, patriotism and sacrifice for country, and omitting the other. She appealed only to "higher" sentiments, to emotions that lay within the "sacred" area. One result, of course, was the rejection of her whole line of argument by some listeners who had been motivated in their bond purchases by the investment theme, and believed that theirs was the more realistic reasoning:

"I believe that bonds should be bought as a result of planning and thought. I try to buy a certain amount each year, over and above each drive. They take the form of an annuity. You get a fair amount of interest. *It's a good sound investment*—the best there is."

But for many people the buying of war bonds is not like buying goods and services, or even like buying railroad bonds or preferred stocks. It is, rather, more nearly analogous to the monetary collections made in church which are thought of not as the wherewithal for the bread and butter of the minister, but rather as an "offering." To tinge such contributions with commercialism would profane the sentiments centered about

---

interests at the same time. When we think of Nationalistic (or sacred) action the idea of self-seeking (or profane) action is excluded, something within us opposes the conflicts caused by the mixture of the two. Nationalistic discourses consist of professions of devotion to the fatherland, exhortations to the same, praise of the fatherland, professions of readiness to sacrifice oneself for the fatherland, stories of the culture heroes or saints of Nationalism who have sacrificed themselves for the fatherland." F. Creedy, *Human Nature Writ Large: a Social Psychologic Survey and Western Anthropology* (Chapel Hill: University of North Carolina Press, 1939), p. 166.

war bonds,[2] which have been termed "sacred" as compared with the more secular attitudes involved in the purchase of material goods for one's self. Patriotic feelings, like religious feelings, are usually, to those experiencing them, beyond the realm of the controversial, and any exhortation to contribute money in either of these fields would be tainted were it spoken of in terms of material advantages accruing to the contributor.

It is not surprising, then, that there is at times considerable resentment of those war bond promotions which offer premiums to the purchasers. In accord with the atmosphere of her campaign, Smith made no such offers. To determine the extent to which such bonuses are deemed compatible with the social symbolism of war bonds, this question was asked of the 978 persons constituting the cross-section poll: "Do you think that it is a good idea to give things to people who buy bonds?" The responses exhibit a clear-cut division, indicating a cleavage in the symbolic overtones of war bonds. Fifty per cent were definitely opposed in principle to premiums, bonuses and other such inducements, and many of the remainder thought it a good idea only for "other people" who might not buy otherwise.[3] The former sentiment is aptly expressed by women interviewed at length: *"You don't sell your patriotism—that's how I feel—I don't want any prizes for my money." "I don't*

[2] ". . . an object is socially sacred when it provokes in members of the group an attitude of reverence and when it can be profaned in the eyes of social opinion, by being connected with some other object." (W. I. Thomas and Florian Znaniecki, *The Polish Peasant in Europe and America* [New York: A. A. Knopf, 1927], p. 1868.) And again: "Since the idea of the sacred is always and everywhere separated from the idea of the profane in the thought of men, and since we picture a kind of logical chasm between the two, the mind irresistibly refuses to allow the two corresponding things to be confounded, or even to be put in contact with each other; for *such a promiscuity, or even too direct a contiguity, would contradict too violently the association of these ideas in the mind. The sacred thing is par excellence that which the profane should not touch and cannot touch with impunity.*" (Emile Durkheim, *Elementary Forms of the Religious Life* [New York: Macmillan, 1915], p. 40.)

[3] For further statistical data on this point, see Appendix C, Table VI.

like bribing people; that's one thing I don't like. If people can
afford to get $50,000 worth of bonds they should get them
without nylon stockings." "You don't have to give away things
with bonds. I think a lot of them make too much of an effort
by offering things, giving things away, kissing people . . . a lot
of people make fools of themselves. You don't have to do that
to buy war bonds." And they definitely approved of the fact
that Smith offered no such rewards. For some, it served further to mark her off from others engaged in the same activity:

> "Sophie——[in making an appeal for bonds] could not have
> meant what she was saying. She had to offer a prize for buy-
> ing—*she couldn't really believe in the mere act of buying,
> then, could she?"*

> "On one broadcast, each star competed to see who could
> offer the highest inducement to buy. *I liked it that Kate Smith
> didn't offer any inducement."*

Such appeals appear to many to be incongruent with the sentiments involved in war bond buying. You do not sell your
patriotism, as the previously quoted informant remarked, you
give it gladly, and you give it not to the person who offers you
the most in return, but to a person who herself harbors such
high-minded sentiments.[4]

The other striking omission from the Smith appeals was the
realistic economic purpose of the war bond drive as an *anti-
inflation measure.* Nothing was said about the rise in consumer
income and the scarcity of goods for civilian consumption.
Listeners were not told of the billions of dollars in excess purchasing power which, if it were not invested, might be tempted
to competitive bidding and to black markets. Thus an oppor-

---

[4] Nonetheless, it appears that premiums (auctions, free tickets for movies,
sports, and other special events) have led to a widespread purchase of bonds.
It would be instructive, though beyond the scope of this study, to learn if
such purchases for a premium led to acute guilt feelings. The commercial
ethos is not easily integrated with "disinterested sacrifice."

tunity for education in vital present-day economics was surrendered in favor of large, delusive statements[5] which of course
others besides Smith were using.

"Buy a bond and bring the boys back."

"You can shorten this war, you know. Each of you in your
heart knows that you can."

In view of the prevalence of such appeals, it is small wonder
that a nation-wide poll at the time of the Third War Loan
found four of every five persons unaware of the possible function of war bonds in curbing inflation. The chief theme implied
that unless people bought bonds the nation would be short of
money to purchase the military supplies needed to win the war.
Thus, in order to utilize a potent motive—the drive to win the
war—the Smith broadcasts indulged in questionable economic
education. For a manipulated public opinion in a fascist state,
where only immediate results need be taken into account, this
might be of little consequence, but in a democracy the quality
of public understanding is not irrelevant.

A minority of our informants, who understood the economic
purposes of bonds, responded unfavorably to Smith's efforts
to import "sentimental and emotional" reasons. It was this
group, generally the more educated informants, who felt that
manipulative techniques rather than rational arguments were
being employed. The appeal to sentiment was identified with
"manipulation." But in place of making Smith the target for
resentment, they bolstered their own self-esteem by pointing

---

[5] The *Minute Man's Manual* for the Fifth Bond Drive recognized the need
for correct information on this point by saying, for the benefit of the volun-
teer bond salesmen: "Don't say 'If you don't buy bonds the boys won't get
equipment,' because half of the people know better!" On this cogently prag-
matic basis, the *Manual* was intended to curb the versatile war bond salesman who would exploit widespread fears and anxieties in his excessively thorough devotion to high patriotic purpose.

to her drive as an unfortunate proof that it "took something like this to get the American people to buy bonds."

If Smith had nothing to say about bonds as sound investments or as a curb to inflation, what did she talk about? The answer to this question goes beyond casual impressions. The content of Smith's broadcasts was analyzed into recurrent themes and the proportion of time devoted to each of these was taken as a crude measure of comparative emphases. As the following chart shows, she dwelt almost exclusively upon six major themes.

CHART I

WHAT SMITH SAID:
TIME DISTRIBUTION OF THEMES

Keynoting her appeals was the theme of *sacrifice* to which Smith devoted fully half her broadcast time. Twenty-six per cent went to stories of the sacrifices of servicemen; almost as much, 20 per cent, to the sacrifices of civilians and 5 per cent to the sacrifice of one civilian in particular, namely, Kate Smith herself.

Sixteen per cent of all Smith had to say dwelt upon the theme of *participation*, setting forth the view that the bond campaign was a common enterprise in which all of us could shuffle off our private egoisms and take part in a massive communal effort. Direct appeals to the families of servicemen accounted for 6 per cent of her broadcast time; a *familial* theme which defined war bonds as a means of getting the boys back home.

Whereas these themes dealt with bond-buying in general, the others were directly concerned with the Smith bond drive in particular. Twelve per cent of her time was devoted to the *competition* theme, which urged listeners to help Smith surpass her earlier bond sale records and to help their own community outdo others in purchasing bonds from her. The *facilitation* theme, accounting for 7 per cent, reminded her hearers of the ease with which they could telephone their bond pledges. And the *personal* theme, in which Smith conversationally referred to her private feelings and aspirations, was casually interwoven into 6 per cent of her broadcasts.

The script writers presumably felt that this distribution of themes would prove effective. How did it actually work out?

The Theme of Sacrifice

Somewhere in *Mein Kampf* Hitler remarks that the strength of a movement must be judged more by the sacrifices it can demand than by the perquisites it can offer. A deep and far-reaching type of human behavior not enough studied by the social psychologist is symbolized by the effort of Prometheus to serve mankind at whatever cost to himself.[6]

---

[6] But the German sociologist Weber had a word for it: *Wertrationalität*, i.e., action arising from the conviction of its unquestionable value, irrespective of consequences. Certain types of sacrifice, heroism, martyrdom exemplify this kind of conduct.

The attempt to fan into active flame the readiness of listeners to sacrifice for the war effort followed three lines. Foremost was *the sacrifice which the boys were making "over there."* The listener was urged to do as much for them as they were ready to do for us.

> "Now they are braving swamps and jungles, risking illness and wounds, pain and death . . . *staking their lives so that you and I may never know the horrors of a blitz or a bombing* . . . nor the tragedy of torture and deliberate starvation. Because our boys' hands are at the throat of the enemy far from home, you and I can sleep in our beds with little fear of sudden death from the skies. Because our boys pin the enemy down far across the world, strange ships do not enter our ports and enemy guns and tanks do not rumble through our streets and across our fields."

Generalities fail to promote empathy and vicarious experiences. To induce these, the Smith broadcasts moved quickly from the abstract to the concrete, from the general to the specific individual.

> "Could you say to Mrs. Viola Buckley . . . *Mrs. Viola Buckley whose son Donald was killed in action* . . . that you are doing everything you can to shorten the war . . . that you are backing up her son to the limit of your abilities?"

The second sort of appeal was based upon *the sacrifices which other civilians were making.*

> "This mother has given one son, and she knows each night when she goes to bed that the other son is doing the same tough job and running the same terrible risk. She knows too that her youngest will soon go away and leave her to fight for his country. *What are you doing compared with what this mother has done?* Are you backing the attack? Are you really, honestly now, in your heart, are you really seeing to it that her sons have the best fighting equipment and plenty

of it? Are you buying luxuries or are you turning those dollars you don't need into war bonds?"

It will be noticed that listeners were thus led to invidious comparisons of themselves with a bereaved parent. Another account—and a most effective one[7]—inviting comparative self-appraisals by listeners was that of a legless veteran of World War I who bought bonds with the money he had been saving for years to buy artificial limbs.

> "Early yesterday morning a man who had lost both legs in the war called in and said he wanted to buy a bond. He wanted to buy a bond with the money he had been saving for years to buy himself a pair of artificial limbs . . . *making the supreme sacrifice*, giving up the dream he had cherished for years, the dream of walking once again. As he said himself: 'My limbs can wait, but this war can't' . . . *What sacrifice are you or I or any of us making that would in any way compare with the self-sacrifice of this magnificent person?* Surely, if a legless veteran can give up his dream of a lifetime, then we can give a little extra money to buy another bond. Don't delay, call Circle 6–4343 and give WABC your order for the biggest bond you can afford, or even more than you can afford. Will you buy a bond?"

Once again, the act of buying a bond is redefined. It is imbued with pathos. It celebrates self-sacrifice. Removed from the plain and unadorned context of transactions in the marketplace, the bond purchase is sanctified as a sacrificial rite.

Never explicit, but insistently in the background, was the third theme of sacrifice. The Smith broadcasts repeatedly reminded listeners that *she herself was making no small sacrifice.* This was no mere indulgence in exalted expressions of senti-

---

[7] The effectiveness of this anecdote is attested by an immediate and sharp rise in the number of telephone pledges following its use on two occasions during the marathon. Moreover, this story was more frequently cited by our informants than any other presented by Smith. The consistency between objective sales results and our interviews support the validity of our interview data.

ment: hers too was a sacrificial act. Throughout the presumed ordeal of an all-day broadcast, reminiscent perhaps of the dogged persistence of our men on the battlefield, Smith too was "carrying on."

> "Hello, everybody, this is Kate Smith again. . . . *Let me tell you it has been a long grind* . . . *sitting here since 8 o'clock yesterday morning* urging each and every American to join in Columbia's great war bond drive and buy at least one bond today and tonight. . . ."

Nor did many listeners object that Smith's sacrifice was hardly to be put in the same category with the first two. Such objections were largely precluded by the intimate and personal quality of Smith's relation to her audience. Many people who were not much moved by the sentimental stories were tremendously impressed by the fact that a sacrificial offering of devotion was being made by Smith right at that moment and almost in their own living room. As we shall see in Chapter 4, her implied sacrifice played a large part in reinforcing the convictions of listeners that she—unlike other war bond spokesmen—was really sincere.

This triangulation of sacrifice, this three-cornered pressure—the boys' sacrifice, other listeners' sacrifice, Smith's sacrifice manifested in the marathon—developed in many listeners a strong sense of unworthiness and guilt. They felt compelled to do something more to keep self-esteem. Only by matching the sacrifices of the other three—converting the triangle into a square, as it were—could tension be relieved. In the words of one informant who seized upon all three components of the sacrifice-triangle in her account of the Smith marathon:

> "I was moved *when she described a boy dying on the battlefield.* She was telling about him from childhood up and telling how a bond could maybe save him. Of course, *I thought of my own boy.* That was the most impressive. *Also the*

story of the legless man. That was a beautiful sacrifice. I'd
have been heartbroken with all the pleading and *knowing
Kate was sacrificing her time* if I hadn't bought the bond."

Then, after the purchase, there was strong evidence of cathar-
sis. Duty had been done and guilt swept away.

"After I called up, I felt good. *I felt that I had done something real on the phone. I got it, and just to bring the boys
home.*"

The Participation Theme

One of the compelling elements of this campaign was the
sense of joining with others in a common effort. Not often in
modern life do citizens experience the togetherness of the old-
fashioned barn-raising, cornhusking, or quilting bee. The war,
of course, and the bond drive as a whole invited participation,
but these were so broad and impersonal that it was hard to
derive much social response and satisfaction from what one
did. The Smith war bond drive provided an occasion for joining in something specific, immediate and dramatic. It provided
surcease from individuated, self-centered activity and from the
sense that the war is too big for the individual's effort to count.
Smith's appeal was couched in terms of "we," "our," and
"us." She brought her listeners in as co-workers.

"We can do it *together*. . . . *We* can put this greatest of all
war bond drives across."

It is necessary to consider this appeal against the background
of psychological isolation which characterizes so much of life
for so many people. Some psychiatric observers have concluded
that neuroses are often due to an extreme separation of "I"
from "they." The psychological isolate feels insecure—the person who thinks and feels and acts in terms of "we" is strength-
ened. Gangs, teams, clubs, lodges, and innumerable other

organizations register our efforts to escape from the egocentric into a sense of social participation. But being enlisted as a group member—even being physically in the presence of others—is no guarantee of social integration. One may still be preoccupied with questions of how he looks, what impression he is making on others, what others think of him, and other egocentric concerns.

Some of the elation which bond buyers reported as they went back to their radios after telephoning an order undoubtedly arose from the sense of having been caught up in a common enterprise. Informants repeatedly testify to the satisfaction of participating in an emotionally significant joint endeavor.[8] It is clearly evident in the remark of a housewife, as she turned from the telephone:

> "Well, Dad, we *did* something. I was part of the show."

Another reports this gratification even more explicitly.

> "We felt that others had been impressed and bought a bond. And the fact that *so many people felt the same way made me feel right—that I was in the right channel.*"

Thus, the bond purchase was not merely an isolated transaction; it was part of an ongoing common enterprise. It represented not merely a stake in the war, but a stake in the communal undertaking directed by Smith. And, in many instances, once having bought a bond, people continued to listen to the radio drive, thus obtaining vicarious satisfaction from what others were doing in the same enterprise. Such continued listening *after* the bond purchase was not "compulsive," but

8 "The most intangible and subtle of incentives is that which I have called the condition of communion . . . It is the feeling of personal comfort in social relations that is sometimes called solidarity, social integration, the gregarious instinct, or social security . . . It is the opportunity for comradeship, for mutual support in personal attitudes." C. I. Barnard, *The Functions of the Executive* (Harvard University Press, 1938), p. 148.

was maintained by the flow of gratification stemming from the success of a joint endeavor in which one was participating.

The Familial Theme

One of the chief loci of emotional relationships in our society is the family. Parental concern for children is firmly institutionalized. It is reinforced by precept, example, myth and sanction. Subject to variation though it may be, the emotional involvement of parents with their children is a firmly rooted and dependable source of motivation. It is imbued with pathos —"that glamour of sentiment which grows up about the pet notion of an age and people and which protects it from criticism."[9] In their management of pathos, Smith's script writers seized upon this culturally emphasized devotion of mothers and fathers to their offspring and related it to other pathos-laden sentiments: sacrifice, courage, death, patriotism.

Nor was the appeal invariably in terms of "your own son"; not all listeners have children or close relatives in the armed forces. Within a context of sympathy, even those listeners without sons in service were to some extent guided into taking the role of another, into responding in the same fashion as a deprived parent or sibling.

"This is Kate Smith again, asking you to buy a war bond in support of the American boys fighting far from home. It's not as if those boys were strangers to us. *They are our sons . . . and our neighbor's sons.* They are the boys from down the road . . . the grocery boy, the office boy, the garage mechanic . . . each and every one of them is a face and a voice that we remember and love. *Those boys are our own boys* and they have the greatest right in the world to our support."

[9] William Graham Sumner, *Folkways* (Boston: Ginn, 1906), p. 180. For the special case of the "pathos of parenthood," see Willard Waller, *The Family* (New York: Cordon, 1938), pp. 462-463.

"That's what war bonds are to every one of us, a chance to buy our boys back. *We've all of us got boys we want back, sons or sweethearts or brothers or husbands or just friends, kids we knew from down the block.* We want them back, all of them, and here, today, is our chance to do something about it."

Listeners repeatedly referred to a particularly effective appeal quoting a man from Utica who had just received word from the War Department that his son would not come back.

"Why, you'd give the whole fifteen million yourself to buy your boy back, if you had it, wouldn't you? I know I would ... I'd be glad to. I'd give everything ... all my money or my health or my own life ... to buy that now. You see, I got a telegram from Washington this morning. *My* boy isn't coming back."

Whatever the validity of the promise that the purchase of war bonds would bring the boys home sooner and safer, it is clear that many listeners were more effectively motivated by this than by any other appeal. No other reason for buying a bond so fully evoked deep-rooted sentiments as that embodied in the slogan—BONDS WILL SAVE LIVES!

This theme, however, had a differential effect on various sectors of the audience. It proved particularly effective among those listeners with a son, grandson, brother or husband in the armed services. Of the sixty informants in this category, 82 per cent spontaneously referred to the bonds-will-save-lives theme, in contrast to only 40 per cent of those with no close relatives in the armed forces. The interviews clearly manifest the differences between the general sense of obligation felt toward "the boys" and the very immediate and personal sense of emotional involvement of parents with their particular boy and his welfare. Such personal relationships converted an abstraction into an emotional reality. The responses of mothers to this theme are typified by reports such as these:

"I wanted to see the war done with and have all the boys back. *My oldest son told me he wouldn't be home any more* and he didn't know where he was going. Kate Smith talked about bringing them back home by buying more bonds *and I made up my mind right away.*"

"I was thinking, 'God knows, *maybe my son will be over there soon.*' The way she talks when she tells this makes you feel you just gotta do something. *She said if we help them, they'll come home quicker, many will be saved.* I said to my friend, 'Kate Smith, she had me in tears on the radio. I'm gonna buy a bond.' Anything we can spare we gotta give."

"I said to my daughter—'buy it off Kate Smith. *Maybe that'll be the bond that will bring your brother home.*'"

These appeals were also meaningful for those with more distant, but emotionally close, kin in the armed forces.

"Her appealing manner and after all, *we all have relatives in the service. It was in their interest that I bought it. I have a number of cousins in the service* and I correspond with all of them. It hit home, the questions she spoke on the radio. She really brought it right to your door. Everyone has someone in the service they want to do something for."

The theme found its most typical and complete expression in portraying the desperate fears and glorious sacrifices of American mothers. Although these sentiments of course affected fathers as well, the Smith broadcasts were in general not directly addressed to men in her audience. "She always mentioned the mother and the family side, sitting home and waiting for the boys," said a male informant who was largely unmoved by her appeals. "I always imagine her appeal as strictly feminine . . . I'm not a Crosby fan, but his appeals seem to be very masculine, man to man."

The sex-linked character of her appeals probably kept the total of bond pledges below what it might have been. For, in many families, it is the husband's role to make decisions on comparatively large investments such as those represented by war bonds. *"You more or less leave the bonds to the man of the family,"* we are told by the wife of a salesclerk. "Saving stamps and collecting fats and scrap—those appeal more to the housewife." *"It's my husband's money, anyway,"* explains another housewife. "He signs the checks, so of course we discuss buying bonds. *He decides when to buy* because he knows when he can afford it."

Had her script writers considered this definition of sex roles, Smith might have substantially increased her bond sales by directing appeals to men. This, it appears, would have served to rescue many lost pledges as well as to initiate additional pledges. For, often, Smith had persuaded women to buy a bond during the course of the day only to have them wait until evening to consult with their husbands who subsequently vetoed the decision. If these persuaded-but-unpledged women failed to swell the total of bond sales, it was because their husbands were not reached by the Smith appeals. "I would have been willing to cut down on food money and other things so that I could buy the bond," explains a devoted Smith fan, "but John wouldn't approve. When he came home, I said, 'Don't you think we ought to squeeze out another bond?' But he said, 'It'll be oversubscribed.' "

The Personal Theme

However, the Smith broadcasts emphasized primarily not the larger social unit, but the direct, intimate you-and-I. There were many expressions of this type in her broadcasts:

"*You* can help *me* send this war drive over the top."

"*You and I* might send this way over the top."

Her public personality and her reputation lead listeners to accept Smith as part of the homely affairs of their daily life.

"It seems that she's sitting in your kitchen and talking to you. *The way it would be with a friend.*"

"She's spontaneous; her speech isn't forced. It's natural, *makes me feel that I'm talking to my neighbor over the washline.*"

The sense of intimacy implied in sharing the kitchen and the washing is further fostered by Smith's use of the form of direct address: "Are *you* buying luxuries? . . ." This "you" was taken by many listeners in the direct personal sense:

"She was speaking *straight to me.*"

"You'd think she was a personal friend. *I feel she's talking to me.*"

The intimacy is carried still further because it goes to the interior, central layers of the personality. While cold logic and pleasant entertainment operate on the periphery of the self, the emotions with which Smith was concerned—love, hate, sacrifice, conscience—penetrate deep into the center.[10] She prepared the way for this approach to the inner recesses of her listeners by offering them first the confidence of her own aspirations.

"Hello, everybody . . . this is Kate Smith again. *Will you help me to make a dream come true?* It's an amazing dream . . . a stupendous dream . . . a dream that may be out of reach . . . but it's a dream I know can be true today *if we all*—everyone of us . . . do our part."

The conviction of Smith's sincerity helped establish this personal relationship. Others may read lines, "Kate reaches the heart."

[10] As we have noted, this is, perhaps, one of the several advantages of the sociopsychological study of real-life situations. Laboratory experiments in social psychology often lack the presumed emotional involvement of subjects in the experimental situation.

"With others, when they say something, you know it's what their agent has written down. With Kate Smith—*she just talks what she thinks.*"

"I don't like the actresses—not like her, so convincing. I don't think that actresses are like that—*too much play-up in their game. You don't go with your heart. She was always calling you back, your heart.*"

Later—in Chapters 4 and 6—we shall try to discover why sincerity was so generally attributed to Smith. The point here is simply that, for reasons yet to be explained, listeners experienced an emotional resonance; their inner self was in tune with that of Smith. Empathy prevailed.

Another technique which served to create this sense of intimacy was to anticipate and speak about possible unfavorable feelings on the part of listeners.

" 'I'm pestering you,' she said, 'but let's put this over for all of us.' "

Such periodic remarks, addressed directly to the listener and commenting on his putative feelings, served to *personalize* the entire appeal and to symbolize utter sincerity. The ostensible clarification of feelings, both Smith's and the listener's, was the very stuff of a heart-to-heart, intimate conversation. As one listener explained:

"I felt she was talking to me. . . . The thing that really made me pick up the phone [to order a bond] was when she said, *'You're probably sick of listening to me, and I'm sick of talking about it, too, but I can't stop.'* I bought it then."

This is communication plus. It is accommodation not only to what is said by the other person, but also to what would normally be left unsaid. The widespread feeling that Smith is "a very understanding person" may well arise from skill in anticipating and verbalizing the unspoken mood of the listener. The fact that she felt free to anticipate negative reactions is of the greatest importance. Only where the ties are strong can one cheerfully recognize and accept hostile feelings. Smith's procedure testifies to her personal security and to the strength of rapport which she presupposed between herself and the listener, a presupposition fully borne out by responses such as this:

> "I cried all day. At the end she always said: 'You may be tired of me, but I've got to keep going.' *I laughed when I heard that—as if anyone could get tired of her.*"

It is not surprising that, with so much emphasis on intimate personal communication, many listeners went to the telephone between broadcasts, expecting to talk directly with Smith herself. As we shall see, for some listeners the desire to speak to Smith on the telephone was actually a motivating factor in the bond purchase. It is true that in one broadcast early in the day, Smith had explained that this would be impossible:

> "I wish I could ask you to telephone me, so that I could talk to each one of you personally and thank you for buying a war bond for America. But I can't do that today. Because during this CBS War Bond Day I'm going to appear on so many CBS programs that I won't have time to talk to each one of you individually."

Some who had missed this warning telephoned, hoping to hear Smith's voice in the answering "Hello." More interesting psychologically were others who converted a wish into an expectation. They knew she was not accessible, but when they called they could not quite rid themselves of a half-hope that somehow the personality that had come with such warmth over the radio into the kitchen would respond to the heartfelt wish of the listener now telephoning as Smith had requested. Just as they knew they could not let her down, they fancied she could not let them down.

> "I really thought Kate would answer the phone. I *just had*

the feeling she would; but I guess it was impossible. I could hear how busy the switchboard was and she was on every fifteen minutes."

In a few instances, the friendly, almost personal atmosphere generated by Smith's broadcasts was felt to contrast sharply with the impersonal and matter-of-fact remarks of those who answered the telephone. The abrupt shift in mood occasioned resentment. A few were led to question the authenticity of the human interest stories Smith told about purchasers of bonds, since the questions asked in taking telephone orders were brief and impersonal.

> "I remember the story about the man who sacrificed his artificial legs. I'd already called up and I wondered how she had got the story, because the young woman I'd talked to *was so businesslike.* Just asked me my name and address. . . . There was another story about an old lady. . . . I was curious where they got those stories because nobody talked to Kate Smith. . . . *It made me slightly skeptical.*"

But for most the sense of rapport with Smith increased after they had pledged their bond. For them, the telephone conversation was merely an interlude, and they returned to the radio to experience a continued communion between their idol and themselves. This was manifest in the previously cited instance of the girl who felt that Smith's song was a response to her purchase. The bond pledge was often experienced as virtually a personal contact with the radio star:

> "My daughter was wildly excited after she had made the phone call, and when some of h   friends came in afterwards, she ran about the room from one to the other crying, '*I bought a bond from Kate Smith!*' "

The Competition Theme

Patterns of competition have long been firmly embedded in our culture. Standardized competitive situations call for and ordinarily elicit increased efforts to reach a goal.[11] Although it was not wholly consonant with the mood of dedication and sacrifice pervading the Smith bond drive to lay great emphasis on the competitive theme, the script writers did not wholly overlook the additional impetus competition could provide. The competitive patterns of the race, the auction, and the surpassing of "records" were all utilized.

> "How about it, the rest of you citizens of cities large and small throughout the country? Have you gotten behind the war bond drive and behind our fighting men *with the same spirit that Anderson, South Carolina, has shown today?* Have you bought bonds to the limit of your ability? And if not, why not?"

And toward the close of the marathon, competition was reduced to Los Angeles and New York City—finally concluding with broadcasts confined to New York to "give New Yorkers a chance to catch up . . ."

> "I was a little disappointed to discover *that the good old town of New York was behind Los Angeles* . . . now we're going to hold the switchboard open to give New Yorkers a chance to catch up to and surpass Los Angeles. Are you with me?"

> "This is Ted Collins speaking to you from WABC, New York. In the mammoth CBS war bond drive conducted by Kate Smith and just concluded, *the city of Los Angeles has bought more war bonds than the people of New York.* Now I'm a New Yorker myself . . . I cut my eye teeth on the Brooklyn Bridge, and it makes me feel kind of sad to see the old home town being outdone even by that fine old city of Los Angeles. So here's what we're going to do . . . we're going to continue the war bond drive here in New York over CBS station WABC . . . giving New Yorkers one more hour in which to catch up with Los Angeles . . ."

[11] See the experimental results summarized in Mark A. May and Leonard W. Doob, *Competition and Cooperation* (New York: Social Science Research Council, 1937), pp. 35–50.

"Come on, New Yorkers. A city located in California is
ahead of New York City. . . . Something's got to be done
about that and that something is a call to Circle 6-4343 where
a bond can be bought in a jiffy."

From time to time, the total amount of bond sales was reported, with the intent of stimulating interest in surpassing
previous levels.

"Why, already, the latest reports from all over the country,
posted under the clock on my studio wall, show that you, as
individual Americans, have bought millions of dollars worth
of war bonds since eight a.m. this morning. If the rest of you
do as well as those who have already phoned in, the total by
midnight will be way over the top. So call that number,
won't you please, and buy your war bond now? Won't you
buy a bond?"

"Help send this drive riding high over its goal—let it be your
notice to Hitler that America stands squarely behind its
fighting men."

These competitive patterns were reflected in the responses
of listeners. Informants who clearly identified themselves with
their community report:

"I've raved about New York all over the country. It's amazing how proud New Yorkers are of being New Yorkers.
When we were stationed out west, we were always glad to
see New Yorkers. She mentioned that the small cities were
doing better than New York, and *I couldn't let New York
down.*"

"I'm a native New Yorker. . . . I felt that New Yorkers
shouldn't let California go over the top. You do care; *you
have a feeling for your own city.*"

Co-operative competition joined Smith with her listeners
in an effort to surpass previous records. This was not a case of
one segment of the audience competing with others, but rather

of all co-operating with Smith to reach a new level of achievement.

> "She said that the last time, she collected—I don't know the figure—and toward the end, when I did buy, *she said she had so much more to go. I felt I was helping her to hit her goal.*"

> "I felt I was helping her. The more she'd get, the better it would be."

The Facilitation Theme

Facilitation of client response has long since been a familiar "principle" in advertising. Obstacles to direct action by the client are to be eliminated or minimized. The Smith campaign repeatedly indicated to listeners the ease with which they could respond: "We've worked it out to make it the easiest thing in the world for every one of you to buy a war bond today. Every one of Columbia's stations, including the one that you're listening to now, has a special war bond telephone number. That's all there is to it . . . Listen for the phone number, jot it down, call that number and order that bond."

Despite the precise four-step instructions—listen, write, call, order—not all listeners found this simple and convenient to do, but most did:

> "I listened all day and the phone was right in front of me. They gave me the number and so I called."

> "It's much easier for me to call up, make out an application and send in a check than it would be to go to the bank."

Quite apart from ease and convenience, facilitation served another psychological function in the bond drive. *The telephone pledge permitted action at the very moment when the listener was most fully motivated by the persuasive Smith.* By reducing to a minimum the interval between the stimulus to action and the possibility of this action, persuasion proved effective in producing an act rather than merely modifying an attitude which might not eventuate in action. Small opportunity was thus afforded to inhibiting factors which might otherwise intervene. This principle of establishing an immediate relation between a command, exhortation or request and the ensuing action has been widely utilized in such diverse areas of social control as child education and military training. A "Lights Out" sign on the wall immediately above the light switch will more frequently produce the desired action than the same sign elsewhere in the room. So, too, the opportunity to convert decision into action was directly provided by the Smith campaign.

The facilitation of response was peculiarly in point for those listeners who experienced a conflict between buying a bond as their conscience demanded and spending the money in some other fashion. They welcomed the opportunity to commit themselves and thus resolve the conflict:

> "Like when you hear someone like Kate Smith, you think 'Oh my goodness, I gotta give, I could do without something.' *Otherwise you put it off. You think someone else will buy today.*"

Some informants expressed the uneasy feeling that the Smith exhortation might prove only temporarily persuasive. Unless action occurred during the interval of persuasion, it might not occur at all. In some instances, listeners telephoned at once precisely because they wished to commit themselves to a bond before inhibiting factors intervened.

> "I decided to call, even though I did not have the money in the house, *so that I would have it in.*"

Indeed, some informants doubted whether a telephoned pledge was a commitment sufficiently binding to overcome the temptation to spend in other ways the money earmarked for the bond. Responsive as they were to Smith's persuasion, they were aware that the state of mind she had created would not be permanent. In such instances, Smith had apparently not modified listeners' prevailing orientations toward bond-buying, but had exerted only an ephemeral and momentary influence. In effect, these informants had small faith in their fulfillment of the pledge, once the impact of the Smith appeals had been dissipated.

> "Well, I would have to mail them a check, call them up, give them my order, wait for the thing to come in the mail. I would rather go to a bank, *I don't like to pledge myself and then have something come in a few days that may make me change my mind.*"

And in a particularly revealing fashion, one informant apparently projected his own doubts onto others:

> "*People* call in and when the time comes, *they* are not in a position to buy it. *They* are moved to buying it, but then *they* can't afterwards. *I* always felt that the way to buy those things, *buying the bonds right on the spot, and then taking no chance of changing your mind.*"

The evidence clearly suggests that if the action Smith was urging could not have been taken so promptly and easily, the response would not have been so great.

The use of the telephone, it may be noted, not only made the purchase of bonds easier; it was a method viewed as particularly consonant with the personal rapport between Smith and many of her listeners. The telephone afforded the simulacrum of personal contact. Signing contracts might be appropriate for impersonal business transactions, but for many this war bond purchase was an expression of personal loyalty to Smith. The give-and-take over the telephone continued the process of communication. The pledge was a personal obligation expressed to Kate Smith's surrogate. "*Over the phone,*" as a housewife summed it up, "*it's like you are giving a promise to somebody.*"

Of the modes of persuasion furnished by the spoken word there are three kinds. The first kind depends on the personal character of the speaker; the second on putting the audience into a certain frame of mind; the third on the proof, or apparent proof, provided by the words of the speech itself. Persuasion is achieved by the speaker's personal character when the speech is so spoken as to make us think him credible. We believe good men more fully and more readily than others: this is true generally whatever the question is, and absolutely true where exact certainty is impossible and opinions are divided. This kind of persuasion, like the others, should be achieved by what the speaker says, not by what people think of his character before he begins to speak. It is not true, as some writers assume in their treatises on rhetoric, that the personal goodness revealed by the speaker contributes nothing to his power of persuasion; on the contrary, his character may almost be called the most effective means of persuasion he possesses. Secondly, persuasion may come through the hearers, when the speech stirs their emotions. Our judgments when we are pleased and friendly are not the same as when we are pained and hostile. It is towards producing these effects, as we maintain, that present-day writers on rhetoric direct the whole of their efforts. . . . Thirdly, persuasion is effected through the speech itself when we have proved a truth or an apparent truth by means of the persuasive arguments suitable to the case in question.

—Aristotle, *Rhetoric*, Book I, Chapter 2

Chapter 4

WAR BONDS AND SMITH IMAGERY: A STUDY IN CONGRUENCE

WE HAVE examined the marathon structure of the Smith bond campaign and have learned something of the way in which it helped fix the response of listeners. We have set forth the themes utilized in the broadcasts and seen how, severally and in composite, they called for feeling and decision and action. Obviously it is not enough to talk about the structure of the campaign or even about the appeals that were made. After all, it was Kate Smith's drive. She was the central figure, and many of our informants felt it right that she should be the central figure. "I was glad *she* was doing it," said one enthusiastic listener. "*She is just the person* to make people see how bad things are." Others may be more fitting than she to endorse a sociological treatise, to serve on the board of a college or as a delegate to an international political conference, but the public imagery of Kate Smith, with all its connotations, is remarkably consonant with the meanings ascribed to war bonds. What was the effect of this congruence on the success of the drive?

Criteria for the Seller of War Bonds

It will be remembered that informants attributed a symbolic, virtually sacred, character to war bonds. In at least this one respect, bonds differ from other objects purchasable in the market place. Does it then follow that, in the public mind, salesmen of war bonds should have particular qualities? To be specific, is it felt that Smith was an appropriate salesman of bonds because she is a good salesman in general, or that she is in some particular way qualified for this role? And if technical competence is not, in the public mind, her principal qualification, by what criteria are her qualifications judged? And how did her assumed attributes enter into the process of mass persuasion?

In an effort to assess the prevailing standards which would be employed in a popular choice of bond salesmen, the following question was put to the cross section sample of approximately one thousand persons: "If you had to choose one well-known person to sell war bonds over the radio, which one of these would be your first choice?" Poll respondents were then confronted with a list of five widely known persons from which to choose. Since this was the initial question in the poll interview, respondents were not aware of any specific interest in Kate Smith on the part of the interviewer. Furthermore, the sequence of names in the list was rotated after each interview to preclude any bias otherwise attributable to position on the list.

Two characteristics of this question should be noted. First, the question was deliberately phrased in general terms. It was largely unstructured. In other words, respondents were not told to make their choice on the basis of any particular criterion; they were free to supply the grounds of their choice in their own terms. In this way, we could determine the tacit or explicit frame of reference which they employed in their selections.

Secondly, the five "candidates" for the bond-selling role were so selected as to enable us to test certain hypotheses about the sociopsychological context in which war bonds are prevalently placed. All five are known to have a large following in the New York area and all had, at one time or another, engaged in a war bond campaign. Two of the five, Betty Grable and Frank Sinatra, were advisedly included in the list as "glamour personalities"[1] from the world of popular entertainment in which Kate Smith presumably also finds her place. Martin Block, a master of ceremonies of a daily popular music program broadcast by the independent New York City station WNEW and a conspicuously successful "radio salesman" of various commodities, was included as a person drawn from the world of advertising and commerce, in which Smith could also be located. Block had been selling bonds over the air in the course of every war bond drive, but his efforts had not been dramatized as a marathon nor did they fit into a context of publicized patriotic endeavor. Finally, Wendell Willkie was selected as a distinguished citizen prominently concerned with affairs of national import. The list of alternatives, then, comprised five persons, all in the public eye, all at one time or another engaged in promoting the sale of war bonds but each differing from the others in his public role.

The tabulation of preferences shows the extent to which Smith outweighs the other candidates as a popular choice for such an undertaking.

Not only did Smith emerge as the pre-eminent choice for this task, but she was selected by almost five times as many persons as her nearest rival, Martin Block. This conspicuous endorsement also appeared when respondents were invited to indicate which of the five alternates they considered least fitted for this role. Whereas Sinatra was considered least appropriate by 35 per cent of the respondents, and Willkie, Block and Grable were accorded this status by 28 per cent,

[1] For the peculiar place of "glamour personalities" in American life, see Gunnar Myrdal, *An American Dilemma* (New York: Harper & Brothers, 1944), Vol. II, pp. 734–735.

TABLE I

"If you had to choose one well-known person to sell war bonds over the radio, which one of these would be your first choice?"

First Choice	%
Kate Smith	62
Martin Block	13
Wendell Willkie	11
Betty Grable	7
Frank Sinatra	7
Total per cent	100
Number of cases	933
No answer	(45)
Total number interviewed	(978)

18 per cent and 16 per cent, respectively, only 3 per cent placed Smith in this position.[2]

All this does suggest that the public image of Smith is endowed with certain distinctive qualities which make her seem peculiarly qualified for promoting the sale of war bonds.

But we have yet to interpret these preferences for Smith. What were the grounds for these choices? Do these grounds help clarify Smith's apparent suitability for the role of bond seller? And do they aid our understanding of the persuasion exercised by Smith in her all-day bond drive?

Examination of the reasons supplied for these selections at once suggests four distinct contexts within which choice was made. Candidates were selected either because of their assumed effectiveness as salesmen or because they were the focus of three types of sentiments.

[2] One might of course raise the question whether this is not due to the greater familiarity with Kate Smith occasioned by her daily broadcasts over a period of many years. An examination of the extent to which she is selected by people who never listen to her, however, shows that familiarity is by no means the primary factor (see Appendix C, Tables I–V).

It is true that somewhat more than half the preferences[3] were based on objective or technical grounds: "he has a large following"; "she has been successful in the sale of bonds"; "he is a good salesman"; "he has proved he can sell anything, including bonds." What these reasons have in common is the perspective of a detached observer arriving at a decision in impersonal terms, resting solely on the presumed effectiveness of a candidate for a specific task. These judgments are wholly in terms of technical efficiency; they contain nothing of sentiment. They embody the attitude of a technician assessing a problem and making his decision solely on utilitarian grounds. They may, of course, be mistaken, but they nonetheless have the context of a "rational" frame of reference.

Such criteria would have been more generally applied, we can assume, if war bonds were not regarded as different from other marketable objects. If the objective were merely to sell as much of a commodity as possible, then of course only the technical criterion of effectiveness would be in point, and more than 52 per cent of these choices would have been made in such terms. Moreover, this criterion varies considerably among the several candidates, suggesting that their specific suitability for selling war bonds (as· distinct from other items) also varies. Significantly enough, it is Sinatra, Grable and Block—the glamour personalities and the professional salesman—who are most often selected on this practical basis, with 59 per cent, 67 per cent and 64 per cent of their respective votes resting on the ground of a large following and sales competence. But only 45 per cent and 48 per cent of the choices of Willkie and Smith, respectively, are based on the impersonal criterion of presumed sales effectiveness. Other attributes, real

[3] For the tabulation summarizing the grounds for choice, see Table II, Appendix C.

or imputed, are evidently required to qualify a person pre-eminently to advocate the purchase of war bonds.

The bulk of other reasons for choice—and they were 48 per cent of the total—were premised on sentiments, and these sentiments fell into three distinct categories. There was, first of all, the

Sentiment of symbolic fitness. Reasons in this category are phrased in moral symbols; they refer to the extent to which the candidate is believed to incarnate the American gospel of sincerity, benevolence, and above all, patriotism. These reasons constitute reaffirmation of American moral values, of American mores. They are not impersonal, detached estimates of what would prove *effective* but of what is *proper*, of what is symbolically fitting. Judgments are couched in terms of what is considered right or wrong, not efficient or inefficient. They are expressions of moral sentiments, not utilitarian appraisals. In these instances, candidates are chosen because they are believed to embody cardinal American virtues:

Patriotism: "She does so much for the war effort."
          "She's a real American."
Benevolence: "She's done so much good for people."
Sincerity: "She's such a sincere person."

Such reasons hark back to the prevailing overtones of war bonds as a national symbol, overtones which we have previously noted in connection with the "sacred" qualities attributed to bonds. War bonds connote blood and suffering and national unity; they are objects of sentiment and emotion and deep feeling. Within this context, a sense of symbolic fitness governs the choice of the person who is qualified to urge the purchase of war bonds. Propriety, not efficiency, becomes the canon for choice.

Patriotism and good will and the moral virtues were the criteria in 23 per cent of all preferences. And it is in this respect that Smith is accorded a marked pre-eminence. A third of the Smith votes are based on her assumed symbolic appropriateness, as compared with only 17 per cent of the Willkie choices. Her role is not that of the entertainer. She is sharply marked off from her more glamorous competitors in the world of entertainment, for Grable is rarely (3 per cent) and Sinatra is never regarded in this light. So, too, the effective salesman, Block, despite his repeated excursions into the marketing of war bonds, is viewed as symbolically appropriate by only 9 per cent of his adherents.

The pre-eminence of Smith becomes even more evident when we examine these choices from another standpoint. We have seen that the criterion of symbolic fitness ranks second only to the effectiveness criterion, 23 per cent (275) of the reasons for choice having this as a basis. More than 3 of every 4 among these 275 reasons were applied to Smith as the person who measured up to this criterion. In short, over and above the technical prerequisites of popularity and assumed persuasive competence, a seller of war bonds must, in the minds of many, have certain qualities and it is Smith, among these alternates at least, who is believed to be so endowed.

The sentiment of personal relationship—a sentiment centering not in cultural symbols but in individuals—was another important basis for choice. In such instances, choices stemmed from the feelings of personal attachment to the selected candidate. "I like him," "I am devoted to her," "I love her voice and singing" are not atypical expressions of the feelings of devotion and identification and followership which prevalently governed these choices.

Eighteen per cent of all choices were couched in terms such as these. Characteristically enough, it is the "glamour personalities" who, if selected at all, are more likely than the others in the list to be selected on this basis. Sinatra and Grable, however extraneous their qualities might appear for the task in hand, ranked high in this respect, with 32 per cent and 20 per cent of the reasons for their respective choices being phrased in these terms. That 25 per cent of the reasons advanced for the selection of Block fall in this same category affords testimony to his personal following among local listeners to his radio program. But for Smith and Willkie this became less significant—16 per cent and 10 per cent, respectively—not because they were without personal followers, of course, but because they had other qualifications which were regarded as important.

There was, finally, the *sentiment of competence in public affairs*—the belief that the most appropriate person to promote the sale of war bonds is one versed in public affairs, who understands the implications of war bonds in realistic terms. Willkie was listed as one of the five "candidates" in the poll because he had identified himself with the war by his quasi-diplomatic world tour and his book, *One World*, and because his service to America at war had been widely reported in radio, print, and film. Certain informants felt strongly that these were important qualifications for the role of bond salesman: "He is serious and has something behind him." "He knows what it is all about." "He has a serious understanding of war problems." "After all, he has the best knowledge of what we are fighting for." In effect, the argument appears to run, the man who has a grasp of the realistic problems of the war is the one best suited to sell war bonds. War bonds are matters of moment, belonging to *la vie sérieuse*, not to the realm of ballyhoo or commerce or entertainment. It does not seem to be assumed that Willkie's experience would enable him to reach a larger total of bond sales, but it was deemed "right and proper" that the role of bond salesman be assigned to one versed in public matters.

It is interesting that this criterion of competence in public affairs should have been so seldom introduced. To be sure, this was the ground in 23 per cent of the preferences expressed for Willkie. But even so, only 3 per cent of all the informants applied this criterion, for Willkie's vote was only 11 per cent of the total. Nearly six times as many votes were cast for Smith as for Willkie. Moreover, the striking fact is that the criterion of symbolic fitness was advanced on 239 occasions for Smith, in contrast to only 27 references to the public competence of Willkie. Clearly, an intimate knowledge and grasp of political realities was not considered paramount by most people. The conclusion seems to be that the execution of important political tasks and the rendering of significant services in the prosecution of the war, however widely publicized, are not enough to transform a person into a symbol of the patriotic virtues. It is revealing that though 14 of the 978 respondents could not identify the ex-presidential candidate Willkie, only one failed to identify the radio star Smith. The dramatized ceremonial symbolism of Smith took precedence over the realistic political activity of Willkie.

The Symbolic Fitness of Smith

As we have seen, Smith exhibits not only the technical advantage of popularity and a record of successful salesmanship but also and pre-eminently a symbolic fitness for the task of selling bonds. Some insight into the components of this symbolic appropriateness is provided by the public images of Smith reported by the hundred perons who were interviewed at length. They talked freely of Smith's bond drive. Implicitly, and at times expressly, they pictured her character, her way of life, her aspirations. And these imagined portraits were invariably charged with evaluations, praising, eulogizing, rarely damning, the images which were for them the "real" Kate

Smith. Table 2 summarizes the array of Smith images obtaining among these hundred informants.

TABLE 2

Public Images of Smith
Projected by Listeners to her Marathon War Bond Drive

Sincere	60
Philanthropic	39
Patriotic	36
"Just plain folks"	26
Guide and mentor	20
Motherly	16
Virtuous	16
Entertainer	7
"A success"	6
Miscellaneous	30
*Number of informants	100

* Each informant characteristically presented several images of Smith, which accounts for the number of images far exceeding one hundred.

From this set of attributes spontaneously ascribed to Smith, it appears that she is not primarily viewed in her role as entertainer. Only 7 per cent of our informants referred to her in this capacity, and the traits with which she was generally endowed by our informants bear little relation to this role. "Sincerity" is foremost among the qualities imputed to her. The 60 per cent of our informants who referred to this trait characteristically did so at length and with considerable affect. Less frequently, but again with marked emphasis, her benevolence and concern for the needy ("philanthropy") and her "patriotism" constitute components of Smith's public imagery.

In an effort to determine the currency of these images, the larger poll group of 978 was asked to select from a list of six attributes that one which *best* describes Smith. "Sincerity" was deliberately omitted from the list since the detailed interviews had suggested that inclusion of this attribute would probably result in the other alternatives being wholly overshadowed in the poll. The other attributes derived from the interviews were translated into readily understood terms and comprised the check list.[4] Table 3 summarizes the responses to the following

TABLE 3

Social Images of Smith Among Different Groups of
Listeners and Nonlisteners to the Smith Noon Program

| Social Images of Smith | Listen to Smith Program | | |
	Regularly	Occasionally	Never
	%	%	%
Very patriotic	44	50	40
All out to help others	21	13	12
Entertainer	7	14	29
Motherly	6	7	4
Able to advise others	9	6	3
Average American woman ..	13	10	12
Total per cent	100	100	100
No. of cases	(165)	(460)	(282)

question—distributed according to the regularity of listening to the Smith noonday radio program: "If you had to describe Kate Smith, which one of these would you choose?"

Although those who have no direct experience of the Smith radio program were more likely to conceive of her primarily in her role of entertainer than were the occasional or regular listeners—the ratio is expressed by the percentages 29 : 14 : 7—even they were chiefly impressed by her other qualities and especially by her patriotism. Patriotism is, of course, the trait prevailingly attributed to Smith by all three groups. So far as other images are concerned, there are instructive differences between regular listeners and nonlisteners. With increasing frequency of

[4] The sequence of attributes was rotated after each interview in order to eliminate the possibility of bias deriving from position in the list.

listening to the Smith program, there is a greater tendency to
conceive of her as a person to whom one might turn for help,
friendship or advice. Thirty-six per cent of her regular listeners have this conception of Smith—21 per cent as all out to help
others, 6 per cent as motherly and 9 per cent as one who is able
to advise—compared with only 26 per cent of occasional listeners and 19 per cent of those who never tune in her program.
These differences help us to understand the extent to which
the radio can mold social images.

All this suggests the anomaly that an entertainer in our
society can take on the attributes ordinarily reserved for the
moral leader.[5] It suggests further that the congruity between
the Smith public image and the connotations of war bonds
is largely a product of the three moral attributes of sincerity,
philanthropy and patriotism which essentially comprise that
image. A more detailed analysis of these attributes as projected
in the hundred intensive interviews should enable us to ferret
out the sociopsychological significance of this imagery for the
process of mass persuasion.

Sincerity Incarnate

The very emphasis on Smith's sincerity is the more striking
when one considers the disenchantment of our informants
with the world of advertising and commercials and propaganda. It is the radio that has brought Kate Smith a host of
devoted adherents and it is the radio that throbs with glowing
praise for brands of cereals, soaps and cigarettes—tributes
which at least some of our informants are convinced neither
the writer nor the speaker really means. In the words of an
urbanite, secure in her skepticism, "I don't believe all the stuff
I hear over the radio. That's for commercial purposes. You
might be able to fool the country people and the backwoods

[5] See the extended discussion in Chapter 6, pp. 145 ff.

people, but not the city people." Radio announcers and featured stars repeatedly assert their enthusiasm for the products of their sponsors; they are said to exhibit a warm personal interest in people they neither know nor take pains to know. Advertisements exploit the passions and fears of the war for ulterior and self-interested purposes.[6] Within this context of commercial duplicity and pretended enthusiasms, Smith is viewed by our informants as the epitome of sincerity and the exponent of truth.

What makes this an extraordinary phenomenon and an instructive problem for research in the molding of reputations is the fact that Smith herself appeared on at least six commercially sponsored radio programs each week. Yet, though she was engaged in apparently the same promotional activities as her opposite numbers in other programs, she was viewed by the majority of her listeners as the direct antithesis of all that these other announcers and stars represent: as the incarnation of sincerity. "She's sincere and *she really means* anything she ever says. It isn't just sittin' up there and talkin' and gettin' paid for it. She's different from what other people are." "You know what she says is true. Next to God she comes when she tells it to you. The way she talks from the shoulder!"

Nor is this belief in her unfeigned and forthright character

[6] A general executive of one of the largest advertising firms in the country sums up the situation since Pearl Harbor: "Copy written on war themes has not been generally thoughtful or inspiring. 'Almost as a pattern,' writes a distinguished advertising man, 'it features glamourous, colorful, schoolboy pictures of zooming American bombers winning the war thanks to Zilch's Bolts and Nuts. Every fat, overloaded war factory seems to be oozing glory and self-esteem . . . The money for this is frankly recommended as better spent on "institutional advertising" than surrendered to the government as excess profits . . . The stomach-turning copy that has resulted will soon dry up the flood.' . . . the chance to *swing on the trapeze of war emotion* has also been grasped by unworthy hands. Many a cheap circular or advertisement in a low-grade paper has urged the public to hoard, through variations of the 'Buy Now' and 'Only 50 Left in Stock' Appeals . . ." Harford Powel, "What the War Has Done to Advertising," *The Public Opinion Quarterly* (Summer, 1942), 195–203.

confined to her behavior in connection with war bonds. It extends to her workaday job. "She's always conscientious, whatever she says. *Even her commercials are interesting and she's sincere about them too*," says one adherent in describing the character of Smith.

Smith is erected into a symbol of sincerity, of truth amid duplicity, of forthrightness amid deceit, honesty amid guile. More often than not, the conviction was expressed that the Smith appeals were spontaneous expressions of her own feelings, that no script writer provided the bridge from her emotions to her messages. "When others say something, you know it's what their agent has written down," it is said, "with Kate Smith, she just talks what she thinks." Or, even if scripts were provided for her, "it wasn't what was written down, or that she was just talking words. It was she herself actually meaning it, *meaning it*, and wanting to have it strike home." Responses such as these testify to the twin skills of the script writers and Smith herself.

The will to believe on the part of those who are insecure and agitated by the deceit, double-dealing and distrust about them converts Smith into a steadfast symbol of integrity. It is a housewife alarmed by the fact that "we have a lot of fascists, Nazis and Americans against our country" who insists that "it's the truth, everything she says. She has a heart of gold."

Within this context appears the conviction of her listeners that she was not paid for her all-day broadcasts during the war bond drive, as indeed she was not. This readiness, in our commercial civilization, to serve without pay was taken as the very touchstone of sincerity and disinterestedness. The swift astonishment with which informants looked upon this disinterested act only expresses their belief in its rarity. "To think that a woman can give up eighteen hours and can stand there and impress people—*and to do this gratis!* I'm positive she wasn't being paid for it. If *she* went on to make a drive, she wouldn't want money for it." And since she was unremuner-ated, reasoned our informants, it follows that what she had to say was genuine, heartfelt and true. "*The words seem to come not from her mouth, but from her soul, from her heart. It wasn't anything she was being paid for.*"

Those few informants who were not quite certain that she was "voluntarily" donating her time looked for reassurance. "I don't know if she was being paid for it or if she had to do it as part of her job or how they work it." "I wondered if she was being paid for it, but I think not."

But many in our society are sensitive, perhaps overly so, to the possibility of chicane, and not all our informants assumed that the absence of direct pecuniary reward was proof of freedom from ulterior benefits. There was a reputation to be won—or maintained—and it was held conceivable that Smith was motivated by a desire for favorable publicity. Perhaps, as one sales manager suggested, projecting the fruits of his own experience onto the all-day bond drive, perhaps "a person that's sincere can be used as a tool by a superior man. I think that's what happened to Kate Smith. As far as she is concerned, she has herself to sell. There's plenty of smart publicity behind her, and maybe a little self-interest too." Or, in the words of another who had never before brought himself to listen to a Smith program, "I'll tell you. I started to think, 'Well, she's thinking of the world, but *she's also thinking a little of Kate Smith.*' It's self-exploitation. There seemed to be something a little more back of it. It seemed to have a little tinge of selfish-ness. It can't be as good as that. She knew she was on the air. *The biggest bucket of water was on the right for Uncle Sam, but there was a little pail on the left for Kate Smith.*"

Others put the onus of their suspicion not on Smith but on her producers. "About the broadcast, I was thinking that in a way they might have had a selfish view, that they wanted to say they got a certain amount of contributions for their sponsors. After all, they are commercially minded. They wanted credit for themselves so that the sponsors would think she is very good and get her another year."

Yet few of our informants voiced such suspicions in the course of protracted interviews. Quite the contrary. Smith's adherents and the more casual listeners to her bond drive alike dismiss the notion that her motives were infected with even the faintest tincture of self-interest. "Most of the time," notes one informant who ordinarily did not listen to Smith programs, "I think this type of record-making is silly, unless it has some definite purpose. But I didn't feel that Kate Smith's performance was a stunt. No ballyhoo. The emphasis was not on her as a person, but on the bond drive. *I was convinced that she was not doing it for personal gain.* She has a large following, in any case. She was really doing it for patriotic and humanitarian reasons." Her admirers were even more explicit. For them there was a profound gulf between the motives of Smith and of others promoting the sale of bonds. *"Take some of these actresses— you think they do everything to sell war bonds. Do they really care about anything but themselves?* But Kate, she's so sincere and she does those things . . . well, the way I feel, it's not for publicity."

Our detailed interviews, then, suggest an abiding faith in Smith's selflessness, a conviction that she, in contrast to others, cares nothing for the publicity and enhanced reputation provided by an all-day bond drive. But how widespread is this view? And how did the marathon bond drive affect the public imagery of Smith? To test the impressions afforded by the intensive interviews through a statistical check, this question was put to the poll respondents: "When Kate Smith goes on the air to sell bonds, do you feel she is thinking about the publicity she will get, about the amount of bonds she will sell, or both?" From the tabulation of responses, it is evident that Smith's motives are prevailingly regarded as wholly free of self-interest.

TABLE 4

Smith's Motives for Promoting War Bond Sales
Ascribed by Listeners and Nonlisteners to Her All-Day Drive

Ascribed Motives	Heard Marathon Broadcasts	Did Not Hear Marathon Broadcasts	Total
	%	%	%
Interested only in promoting bonds	86	73	80
Interested in publicity for herself, as well*	14	27	20
Total per cent	100	100	100
No. of respondents ...	536	411	947

* This category includes those who felt that she was *primarily* concerned with publicity *and* those who felt she was *also* concerned with promoting bond sales. It thus represents a *maximum* estimate of the proportion of persons who believed that she was to any degree interested in publicity.

Four of every five persons were convinced that Smith was interested *only* in the promotion of bonds. Only a scant 3 per cent felt that she was *primarily* interested in the resulting publicity. These figures become even more revealing when we note that a larger proportion of those who actually heard Smith that day were convinced of her disinterestedness than of those who did not. This appears to indicate that the marathon bond drive enhanced the public conviction of her sincerity. But we must recognize the possibility that her devoted adherents, for whom her sincerity was unquestioned, would be more likely to have heard the marathon broadcasts. Therefore, to determine whether the marathon broadcasts did in fact *extend* this belief, we must compare regular listeners to her programs with those who are not her fans.

CHART II

This chart illustrates one phase in the building of a public image. A major by-product of the Smith war bond marathon was the spread of belief in her altruism. A larger proportion of those who heard her marathon than of those who did not believed that she was engaged in this effort for wholly altruistic and disinterested reasons. This holds true for her fans, for occasional listeners to her noonday program, and for those who never listen to her program.

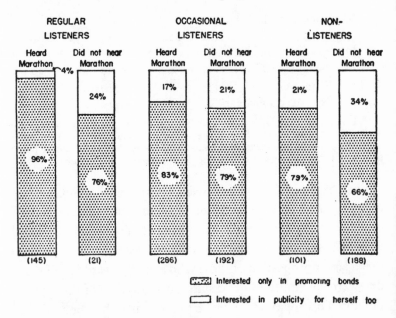

Within each group, a significantly larger proportion of persons who heard the marathon broadcasts were convinced of Smith's disinterestedness. This is as true for her devoted fans as for those who do not listen to her regular programs at all. In other words, *we have caught for a moment, as with a still*

camera, a snapshot of Smith's reputation of disinterestedness in the process of being even further enhanced. We have frozen in mid-course the process of building a reputation. In substance, we have here isolated the effect of "propaganda of the deed" in the molding of a public image. From our data, one can foresee how Smith's listeners will cite this event as more concrete evidence of her utter selflessness and patriotism. Whatever her intentions, the marathon bond drive did indeed contribute to the public image of Smith-the-patriot.[7]

The Marathon: Validation of Sincerity

We have shown that the marathon definitely increased the proportion of listeners who were convinced of Smith's sincerity, but we still do not know how this happened. It is at this point that the intensive interviews, with their often ingenuous and always informative details, permit us to interpret the statistical results of the poll. And it is at this point, also, that our analysis of the marathon structure in Chapter 2 suggests avenues for interpretation.

Persuasive oratory takes time to develop its effects. Hitler often spoke for two hours or more, working up himself, as well as his audience, to a fanatical pitch. One cannot wring tears from an audience without building up to it. This is a very real handicap for the spot announcer on the radio who has but a scant minute or two, for an abrupt and unpresaged display of emotion is likely to prove unconvincing. But Smith suffered from no such limitation the day of the marathon, as a result of the cumulative nature of an intermittent flow of appeals

---

[7] This belief in Smith's disinterestedness was equally current among men and women. It proved even more marked among the presumably less critical: contrast the 85 per cent of those who had no high school education with the 73 per cent of college graduates who entertained this belief. And yet, as our figures indicate, the large majority of persons on each educational level held fast to the conviction of her sincerity.

which, as we have seen, were bound into a single time-configuration. Her appeals were linked into a cumulative series and, as they listened, her audience became increasingly impressed with her sincerity. "She tore my heart down . . . her voice gets you all the time. She bore me down. She always said something about bonds on every broadcast, put something in. But this time, she put it so convincingly, she was going on and going on, this time she got me." The sheer recurrence of her appeals enabled Smith to continue from the level of effective response which she had previously reached. "Her voice improved with each hour, got more appealing with each hour. She put more of herself in it."

But the cumulation of affect and emotion was not the major function of the marathon broadcasts. Above all, *the presumed stress and strain of the eighteen-hour series of broadcasts served to validate Smith's sincerity.* The deed, not the word, furnished the ostensible proof. Not merely the content of her messages, but the *fact* of the all-day drive, believed to be unique in radio history, was taken to testify to her distinctive willingness to serve. For many listeners, the direct testimony of their senses was indubitable evidence, for "*she was on all day and the others weren't. So it seemed that she was sacrificing more and was more sincere. She was making an extra effort, so it was a more personalized feeling than with the others.*"

To be sure, the Smith talks were focused on the sacrifice of soldiers or civilian bond buyers, but, as we have seen, there were frequent indirect allusions to the all-consuming task in which she was engaged. Listeners might question whether she was not unduly dramatizing herself, but they could not escape the incontrovertible evidence that Smith was devoting the entire day to the task. Solicitous reports by her coadjutor, Ted Collins, reinforced the emphatic concern for the strain to which Smith was subjecting herself. "I felt, I can't stand this any longer," recalls one informant, "Mr. Collins' statement about her being so exhausted, affected me so much that I just couldn't bear it." And another, projecting herself into the vividly imagined situation of fatigue and brave exertion, reports: "Ted Collins came on and said, 'It's late but Kate insists that she is going to be on the air until daylight if necessary.' *My heart ached for her* and I was just hoping that she had a couch to lie on there."

The event had all the atmosphere of determined, resolute endeavor under tremendous difficulties. Some could detect signs of strain—and courageous persistence. "Her voice was not quite so strong later, but *she stuck it out like a good soldier.*" Anxieties grew. "I was praying that she would hold out." Her devoted fans, in particular, conjured up visions of acute emotional and physical distress: "I thought she must be very tired and exhausted, because I heard her say, 'If my strength holds out, I'll be here till two a.m.' *I was thinking to myself, she must be pale and tired now.*" Listeners who identified themselves with the sacrificing Smith were sensitive to cues of the ordeal and shared her distress. "She seemed to be getting exhausted. In the early afternoon, it seemed as if there were tears in her voice. My feelings were that she was overexerting herself. It seemed she was doing so much. I wonder: did she lie down? *She sounded so tired, her voice was trembling. I had tears in my eyes.*"

There were some, of course, like those in the barroom described in Chapter 2, who looked impersonally on the marathon broadcasts as little more than an endurance contest. Others, though initially skeptical or even hostile, modified their attitudes as the apparently real-life drama unfolded. "As time went on, I did begin to realize the nuisance value of certain types of advertising, and *gradually my feelings turned to a sort of grudging admiration.*"

It would seem, then, that the marathon broadcast took on the attributes of a sacrificial ritual. Its emotional overtones were not unlike those of the hunger strike or of the Indian Satyagraha (passive resistance). The presumed ordeal became a symbol of the ordeals to which our fighting men are subjected. (Recall the informant's ". . . she stuck it out like a good soldier.") Smith escaped from any context of Hollywood luxury and ease to put on the hairshirt of the ascetic and martyr. Comfort of self was sacrificed to a sanctified cause. Among the more highly educated informants as well, generally critical and quick to detect buncombe, this propaganda-of-the-deed was not infrequently accepted as evidence of Smith's sincerity. "I was wondering if I was the kind of sucker to fall for a good sales talk," says a college graduate, adding, "I did want to help Kate Smith *as long as she was putting so many hours into it.*"

For an understanding of the process of persuasion, the most significant feature of these responses to the marathon is the effectiveness of this progaganda-of-the-deed[8] among the very people who were distrustful and skeptical of mere exhortation. Smith did not insist on her personal sacrifice; she merely interlarded her broadcasts with brief and indirect allusions to her all-day stint. (For every reference to Smith's own sacrifice, there were six to the sacrifice of our fighting men and five to the sacrifice of civilians.) For the most part members of the audience were permitted to draw their own conclusions from *the action*—her recurring appearances before the microphone throughout the day. Researches in various fields of mass communication—radio, print, films—have shown that such "propa-

[8] Perhaps the most dramatic use recently of persuasion-through-the-deed was President Roosevelt's tour through New York City in an open car during a driving rain, an act which directly countered the whispers of his "failing health." It is likely that this act proved far more effective in curbing these rumors than a series of public reassurances by his physician. (This note remains as written in 1944.)

ganda of facts" prove effective where verbal exhortations are rejected.[9] Some segments of our society exhibit a pervasive distrust of what is viewed as propaganda. In these circles, propaganditis has reached epidemic proportions, so that any statement of values is likely to be discounted as "mere propaganda" and all direct expressions of sentiment are suspect. In contrast, for the cynically disposed, and, of course, all the more for the innocent of mind, the propaganda of facts has confidence value. It elicits a ready confidence registered in the folk saying that "actions speak louder than words," a phrase which overlooks the ease with which acts, as well as words, can be manipulative in character. The propaganda of facts, like any other tool, can be abused as well as used.[10] The pseudo-act, in other words, can supplant the act and can be as effective as if it were genuine. The Smith ordeal was taken as an action which attested powerfully to her sincerity and patriotism.

Viewed as a process of persuasion, the marathon converted initial feelings of skepticism and doubt among listeners into a reluctant, and then, a full-fledged acceptance of Smith's integrity. The successive broadcasts served as a fulfillment in action of a promise in words. The operation of this propaganda of

[9] Paul F. Lazarsfeld and Robert K. Merton, "Studies in Radio and Film Propaganda," *Transactions, The New York Academy of Sciences*, Series II, 6 (1943), pp. 58–79, esp. pp. 75–79.

[10] "Several observers have commented on the Nazi 'stage-managing' of reality. It is reported, for example, that prior to the invasion of Belgium, a German officer made an apparently forced landing in Belgium. On his person were found plans for an invasion quite unlike that actually intended. Or again, there is the case of the first night bombing of Berlin. It is said that the Nazis planted reports of great destruction in Berlin in Swiss and Swedish newspapers, accrediting these reports to the British. These accounts were rebroadcast over the German domestic radio and the local population was invited to look at the actual damage and *see for themselves* that the reports were untrue. In this way, probably, many people could not escape the conclusion that the British had lied. The effect of this type of *self-indoctrination* was probably considerably greater than if the German radio had directly denounced the veracity of the British." *Ibid.*, p. 78. For extensive discussions of this technique, see Ernst Kris and Hans Speier, *German Radio Propaganda* (New York: Oxford University Press, 1944).

facts is clearly reflected in the report of one informant who experienced this progressive change in attitude.

> "At eight in the morning, she said, 'This is Kate Smith and I'm going to talk to you every fifteen minutes as long as my voice holds out.' I thought, 'Hmph, she hasn't begun talking yet and she's talking about quitting already.' *I've been getting fed up with all the big names getting all the credit for war work.* I thought, 'Here's another. Kate Smith will do a little talking and get credit for being a wonderful war worker.' So I turned on my faucet and I ignored the rest of her talk at that time. In the beginning, I thought she regarded it as a job she had to do. *Later she seemed to be really sincere. My reaction changed favorably, not because of what she was saying, but because she was still at it.* After about the eighth appeal I began to listen more whole-heartedly. Then I got furious at myself that a little thing like her interrupting one of my favorite programs should have annoyed me. I laughed at myself too. I thought, 'You don't like Kate Smith, and here you are staying in to hear her.' *After listening to her for so long I thought she had integrity. She kept her promise.*"

The marathon, then, reinforced the appropriateness of Smith as a salesman of war bonds. By this act, she *earned* the right to speak. She was not subjected to resentment leveled at others who lack the moral authority to make demands in the name of the nation, a resentment epitomized in the words of a Navy officer who wrote (in a letter to *Time*, published May 18, 1942): "Why do the phrases sound cheap and banal, proper objects for derisive laughter? *Because the radio announcers . . . have not earned the right to utter them.*"

It must be remembered that the incessant demands to buy war bonds, demands couched in terms of moral obligation, invite feelings of guilt and personal inadequacy among those who privately feel they are not living up to these obligations.

This is the very setting in which animosities will be directed against those who provoke this sense of guilt, unless the instigators of guilt are themselves believed to be above reproach. If the persons advocating the purchase of war bonds are not to become the target of resentment and hostility, then they must be endowed with the moral authority to make these demands. Those who struck out defensively against an exacerbated sense of guilt deflected hostility from Smith, whose moral authority was validated by the marathon and the public images of her self-denial.

Repeated bond campaigns were likely to build a sense of guilt particularly among those unable to meet the demands made of them. For example, the mother of a son in service cries out against the insistent and profoundly disturbing claims which she could not satisfy: "Well, sometimes I think they really overdo it. Well, askin'—well, the first, second, and third loan went over alright—*when you live on a small income and you can't do these things*, it's annoying. *It gets on your nerves.* When you hear them sayin' those things, you figure, *what do they want from me, my blood?* [Very excitedly] I guess if you have the money, it doesn't bother you. *It's too much sometimes.*" Moved by this sense of not having met endlessly reiterated demands, she goes on aggressively to indict the radio announcers who have *not* validated their "right" to make these demands: "Honestly, when you hear that man [radio announcer] on the radio telling you to buy bonds, you'd like to examine him. He's talking—maybe he's a flagwaver! *How do I know what he does? Maybe he doesn't do anything. Maybe he just sits in a nice easy chair, yapping it out! He gets paid for it, but how do I know if he buys?*"

From this nice calculus of sacrifice, Smith emerges unscathed. She had won the right to speak, for, in the words of the same informant, "She's a good American, giving her time for nothing. *When the girl was giving up her time, I felt it was no more than right that everyone should help her put over the drive* . . . 8–8:30 a.m. She was on every ten minutes. 10 a.m. The girl was still on. Was I surprised! 12 noon: Again—and the girl was still on. And all evening after supper. I listened until 10 p.m. . . . . It just gets under your skin and you have to buy."

Quite apart from affording the possibility of reiterated messages, then, the marathon reinforced a prevailing conception of Smith as singularly appropriate for the task of advocating the sale of bonds on a mass scale. The *act*, interpreted as indubitable proof of her willingness to sacrifice, persuaded those who resisted the word. The assumed sacrifice endowed her with moral authority and legitimized her claims. In effect, then, the by-products of the marathon entered as fully into the process of persuasion as its main technical advantage of providing for the reiteration of appeals.

Yet it was not the marathon alone that induced the prevailing emphasis on Smith's sincerity. The marathon merely reinforced this image, current long before the bond drive. Contributing to this belief was Smith's well-established reputation for benevolence and generosity.

Doer of Good

Observers of the American way of life, from Bryce through Sumner to Myrdal, have repeatedly noted the central place of humanitarianism in the American creed. This is not to deny that humanitarian codes are often honored in the breach. It is only to say that, in general, the doer of good who moves in well-established channels of benevolence and philanthropy and charity will gain a warm response from many Americans. It is precisely by conforming to these humanitarian mores that Smith establishes a public readiness to accept her further activities as indubitably sincere. Well before the marathon as a crowning example of her own good deeds, she had established a widely held stereotype of Smith-the-benevolent. For her adherents, then, the marathon was merely one more occasion in a long line of good works. "I think she was being true to color. *It's the sort of thing you'd expect Kate Smith to do, and she did it.*" "*You know she does an awful lot of things*, singing for the boys in the last World War, and for infantile paralysis. She always seems to me so sincere—there's that word again!"

Quite apart from Smith's intentions, it becomes evident that her publicly heralded record as a doer of good invited a stereotype which made her seem peculiarly appropriate for advocating the purchase of war bonds. Through a cumulating propaganda of the deed,[11] she had acquired a backlog of consistent public images in which her role as entertainer became second to her role as philanthropist. And it is this role that makes her readily appropriate for a fresh act of disinterestedness as a purveyor of war bonds. "*She is so good.* She sacrifices a lot. Didn't she sing to help the poor? Didn't she buy an airplane and present it to the government?"

Informants cite a considerable array of Smith's benevolent actions as evidence of their belief that it is eminently "fitting" to have someone who is herself a benefactress, a disinterested doer of good, ask that we buy war bonds. "She is so for humanity," it is said. Witness the toys she has collected for orphans; her assistance to performers of a bygone day; her donations to Father Flanagan's Boys' Town; her public appearances in the interest of the Red Cross, the infantile paralysis fund, and other varied charities; consider her songs for the boys in camps and in hospitals and, not least, the "Kate Smith

---

[11] By this time, it should be clear that we are not passing judgment on Miss Smith's motives (which are inaccessible to us) when we allude to "propaganda" of the deed. We refer only to the effect of these actions upon popularly held images of Smith.

bomber" which, our informants maintain, she donated to the government.[12]

Nor do informants express suspicions of one whose good deeds are so widely heralded. For Smith herself does not explicitly call attention to her benevolence. The truth will out, in spite of herself. As one informant puts it admiringly: "She gives in such an offhand way—doesn't make a fuss about it." This is the tactic of inadvertence. The accounts of her benevolence slip out inadvertently, as a by-product of some other discussion and without any manifest concern for the building of a reputation. Casual mention of Smith's latest excursion to army camps and hospitals is seized upon by her adherents. Or a story in a popular magazine supplies inside information about her unostentatious gifts to a poor family or her patriotic endeavors. *"You read little articles about her, but she never advertises herself.* Like when she paid for a band to go to the camps. She does it out of the goodness of her heart. I don't think she does it for a boast." And, the same informant goes on to add, "I never knew she bought a bomber. I suppose most people didn't know." Then, innocently referring to the source of her private information: *"I heard her one day* when she said *her* bomber was lost and everyone should pray for the boys who were in it." Such *indirect* allusions to "her" bomber, enmeshed in a fabric of pathos, were cited by other informants as testimony to Smith's benevolence: "I believe she's sincere about what she says and does. The other day, I heard her talk about her bomber that was lost. And she prays to the Lord

[12] In an earlier broadcast, Smith had alluded to the loss of "her" bomber in action. This was at once taken by her fans to mean that she had purchased a bomber and donated it to the government. The public image of Smith is so well established that the bomber was taken as one more instance of her good works. In point of fact, as she indicated, Smith had merely been invited to christen a bomber which had been named after her. Only in this sense was it "her" bomber. This illustrates the way in which her fans structured an unclear situation by imposing their conceptions of Smith upon it.

that they are safe. *Now why should she do that if she didn't buy it and if she wasn't good?*"

But the mere performance and widespread recognition of benevolent deeds are not sufficient to build a reputation for humanitarianism. The doer of good must also escape the Lady Bountiful role. To begin with, the belief in her integrity and sincerity rests on the fact that she participates directly in her humanitarian enterprises. Hers is no casual bestowing of funds in a fashion which does not bespeak personal involvement: "You don't find many single women who do something today. *They just give money away and are finished with it, but she actually does something.* . . . She is so for humanity. Today the single woman thinks all of career and career . . . [scornfully] *. . . I see them, just put on their diamonds and fur coats.* They just think of themselves. They think they give a house when they give a dollar away."

In addition to participating personally, Smith takes the edge off her benefactions by insisting that she too is essentially one of the plain folk (as we shall see in detail later). Benevolence coupled with social distance breeds resentment, rather than appreciation. Other celebrities are frequently resented as condescending and aloof, but Smith's simple language, homey anecdotes, and plain manner have established quite a different image of her. "She is," we are told, "just like your neighbor next door." She thus becomes genuinely identified with the people she helps. She is a neighbor lending a hand, not a wealthy woman or self-interested star out "to assist the needy." In terms of income, Smith may belong to the upper strata, but she manages to escape psychological identification with them. She is a member of the in-group, as informants in effect tell us. "We're working class, *we're poor class.* . . . *She's not a disto-cratic* [aristocratic] *person.* She's more for the poor class. And for the boys." Economically disadvantaged fans, in commenting on Smith's generosity, go on to speak in circumstantial detail of how like her they themselves are. She provides a prototype of benevolence with which they identify themselves. "I just listen to her every day. I listen to stories and then I hear her. *I'm a person too, you know. I'm good. I never turned a poor man away from the house.* Would you believe it, when my husband was out of work and I had sixteen cents to my name, and a poor man came to the house one morning—he looked awful—and I gave him my last sixteen cents and told him to buy some coffee." We shall comment again on this transcendence of feeling across class lines in our discussion of Smith's "resolution" of personal conflicts of her adherents.

There is, then, a kind of virtuous-circle relationship between Smith's reputation for sincerity and her reputation for benevolence. Each reinforces the other. Her charitable *acts* are held to testify to her sincerity. And, in turn, because of belief in her sincerity, her charitable appeals are taken as genuine evidence of her benevolence. Thus the stories she tells of others' deprivations serve not only to induce immediate response in the listener but remain as a halo about Smith herself.

A variety of factors, then, converge to produce the public image of a benevolent Smith—published accounts of her charities; inadvertent and casual radio references to her contributions; expressions of her identification with other plain people; the halo transferred from the kind of people she talks about to Smith herself—all these contribute to her established reputation as a doer of good.

In the course of our intensive interviews we found a few who doubted her sincerity and some who objected to her use of patriotic symbols, but none who questioned her benevolence. Precisely because she has become a prototype of altruism, Smith becomes an appropriate person to urge the purchase of war bonds. She symbolizes a harmony of sentiments. When people are asked to give in a "humanitarian cause," they want the request to come from someone who has acted in accord with the humanitarian mores. She has validated her right to speak.

Patriotism: Symbol and Fact

Whatever else war bonds may mean to Americans, they are invariably associated with patriotism. A war bond rally without American flags and bunting and the national anthem would be a ceremony without the ritualistic apparatus. And in similar fashion, the bond rally speaker who is felt to be peculiarly suited for the occasion must be distinguished for love of country.

It is significant, then, that apart from sincerity, the attribute most often ascribed to Smith is patriotism. Almost half of the thousand New Yorkers who were asked to select the one of six traits which best describes Smith seized upon her patriotism. She is a flag-wrapped symbol, inseparably associated with a cluster of acts taken to express her abiding patriotism.

But what did informants mean by Americanism and patriotism in this connection? What is implied by the fact that only three of the 101 individuals who selected Wendell Willkie as an appropriate person to sell war bonds referred to his "patriotism" as a basis for their choice? That, in contrast, 52 persons (9 per cent of 574 votes) selected Smith on this basis? To be sure, those who did select Willkie admired his grasp of issues vital to the welfare of the nation, but to most there seemed no relation between patriotism and his efforts in behalf of national welfare. It is not these large, sometimes technically difficult, and always comprehensive matters which are commonly construed as patriotic activity. Problems of public policy appear remote and impersonal and unrelated to the stuff of daily life. Instead it is the dramatized event—the songs for wounded soldiers in hospitals, the excursions to army camps, the expression of patriotic sentiments in "God Bless America"—it is the direct, limited graspable act, fitting into the immediate experi-

CHART III

This chart indicates another by-product of the war bond marathon. This highly dramatized event furthered the public image of Smith as *primarily* a patriot rather than an entertainer. When asked to indicate which attribute best described Smith, those who heard the marathon were more likely than those who did not to select "patriot" rather than "entertainer." This holds true for fans, occasional listeners, and those who never listen to her noonday program.

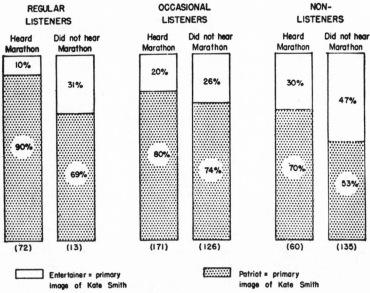

ence of millions of Americans which is simply understood and readily construed as patriotic. Individuals do not commonly identify and experience broad social issues; but they have sons and brothers in army camps, they have known in illness the comfort of a cheering word, they have thrilled to the resounding phrases of patriotic songs. And it is through participation in activities close to the actual experience of most Americans that Smith creates an atmosphere of patriotism and national feeling.

Here, again, Smith's marathon drive serves as a case in point. Just as we have shown that the marathon served to extend public belief in her sincerity, so it can be demonstrated that it spread her reputation as a patriot. As is evident from Chart III, hearing the Smith marathon increases the currency of her image as a patriot among various sectors of the radio audience.

There are some, of course—those few, for example, who lauded Willkie's efforts to help shape the policy of the country in war and the peace to come—for whom the public display of appropriate sentiment is not patriotism and with whom Smith's symbols of patriotism carried little weight. "Frankly, the person that Kate Smith is doesn't appeal to me," says a housewife who discounts the symbol and seeks the fact. "Every time I hear her I think of a great big American flag. I can see how she appeals to certain people, but *I want to dig deeper*." But for the majority, patriotism *is* the symbolic expression of loyalty and seems to have little to do with voting, paying taxes, being concerned with community or national welfare, the treatment of minority groups, national or international policies.

One stylistic device probably has had much to do with building the image of Smith-the-patriot. This is her propensity for the word "America." The words "America," "American," "Americans" occur 45 times in 36 broadcasts covering a total of about one hour of her actual speaking time.

"The dream is as big as all America."

"Thank you for buying a bond for America."

"My personal appeal for each and every American . . ."

"Stuff Americans are made of . . ."

"Whoever he was, he was an American."

"What one American can do . . ."

"Everything a young American should have . . ."

And so, speaking to all of us for all of us, Smith becomes a spokesman for the nation in a crescendo of patriotic affirmation:

"These folks I just mentioned are only a few of the *Americans* who are making this CBS bond day count for the boys over there. Just a few of the *Americans* who realize what buying a bond means. . . . I believe if all of you could hear the reports of bond sales coming in, and know the thrill of feeling *America* backing the attack, you'd get in there even stronger. No *American* who knows what it means to live in this free land . . ."

Thus far, we have been considering Smith's *speech* behavior —*what* she says—in relation to the current imagery of her patriotism and sincerity. But intimately related to all this is her voice, with its intonations and cadences, its rhythms and pitch, its intensity and pronunciation. Groping for a distinctive and specific "cause" of their belief in Smith's genuine patriotism, informants refer to her voice as manifestly sincere. (This does not prevent many from anatomizing Smith's sincerity, characteristically locating it, not at any point in her vocal apparatus, but in her "heart and soul.") "I know she was in earnest because the way she talks. That can't come just from the mouth, that comes from the heart," says a housewife who had resisted the appeals of other radio orators. And another: "She puts her whole heart and soul into it. It's in her speech. When she asks for anything, she gives it everything she's got. *It's in her tone. There's something in it that begs and asks; it's hard to explain.*" And from a third, who excludes the content of Smith's talks altogether: "She's so sincere. *It's her tone, no matter what she says, you sit there and listen.*"

To be sure, these comments are consistent with the verdict of Cantril and Allport that "psychologists will do well to notice that 'sincerity' is an unmistakable attribute of voice. Whether to sound 'sincere' must correspond to inner conviction or whether it may be a pose is another question."[13] But this still leaves indeterminate the ground on which one voice is judged as sincere and another not. A clue is provided by the social psychologist, George H. Mead, who points out that the impression of sincerity occurs when the listener becomes aware that the speaker is using verbal symbols which evidently affect himself as he intends them to affect the audience. Sincerity provides for a mutual experience. And it is the image of Smith responding to her own words that endows her pleas with sincerity: "what penetrated at that time was her begging you to buy bonds which sounded as if she had gotten down on her knees and had tears rolling down her cheeks." Or, in a phrase reminiscent of Mead's formula for sincerity: "She talks as *if she herself is going through all that. What she said she really felt herself;* you knew she wasn't just reading script." It is not the mere content but the overtones that contribute to the total effect of Smith's talks.[14]

[13] Hadley Cantril and Gordon W. Allport, *The Psychology of Radio* (New York: Harper & Brothers, 1935), p. 72. They go on to observe that in the case of a "popular radio philosopher," "we confess our surprise at hearing him speak so convincingly over the air just after analyzing for us so cold-bloodedly the structure of his program. Something for everyone plus 'sincerity': an almost perfect psychological formula for the type of broadcast that attempts to reach a large population."

[14] See in this connection the comments of Harry Stack Sullivan. "The person who speaks over the wireless is addressing a presumptively great number of people. . . . If he is at all expert, his voice communicates the impression *not* of someone reading something aloud *but of a rounded personality talking to one.* In this fact, there lies a field of investigation of very great importance. The study of the personalizations [public images] *of the radio speaker,* as they appear in persons who habitually listen to him, is certainly a fruitful approach to an understanding of the non-verbal communicative aspects of the voice." H. S. Sullivan, "Conceptions of modern psychiatry," *Psychiatry,* 3 (1940), 17n.

It is only an apparent paradox to say that these responses to Smith's voice are not based solely on her voice alone. Listeners' impressions of her quality of voice are undoubtedly affected not only by what she says, but also by their previous images of Smith. Her voice itself becomes "patriotic," as a result of its repeated exercise in patriotic contexts.[15] "She has such a *sincere, patriotic* voice." Thus the patriotic sentiments of her erstwhile theme song are transferred onto her voice: "I knew she was quite patriotic from the way she sang '*God Bless America.*' And, as far back as I can remember, *when you think of Kate, you think of America.* Didn't President Roosevelt ask her to sing 'God Bless America' in *This Is the Army?*" The vehicle—voice—is identified with content—patriotism—and Smith is endowed with a "patriotic voice."

Thus we see that a radio star can build a reputation for patriotism as well as for benevolence by talking a great deal in terms of the appropriate symbols. Yet in each case the words are reinforced by things the star has actually done. The currency of talk is accepted because it is backed up by the gold of conduct. The gold reserve, moreover, need not even approximate the amount of currency it can support. This is particularly true for persons such as Smith whose reputations are not being systematically challenged by counterinterests. In a later chapter, we shall comment further on the favorable position of the person who can be an unopposed symbol.

[15] "It is a well-known law that the sentiments aroused in us by something spontaneously attach themselves to the symbol which represents them . . . This transference of sentiments comes simply from the fact that the idea of a thing and the idea of its symbol [or vehicle] are closely united in our minds; the result is that the emotions provoked by the one extend contagiously to the other." Emile Durkheim, *Elementary Forms of the Religious Life*, p. 220.

Socrates. Oratory is the art of enchanting the soul, and therefore he who would be an orator has to learn the differences of human souls—they are so many and of such a nature, and from them come the differences between man and man. Having proceeded thus far in his analysis, he will next divide speeches into their different classes:—'Such and such persons,' he will say, 'are affected by this or that kind of speech in this or that way,' and he will tell you why. The pupil must have a good theoretical notion of them first, and then he must have experience of them in actual life, and be able to follow them with all his senses about him, or he will never get beyond the precepts of his masters. But when he understands what persons are persuaded by what arguments, and sees the person about whom he was speaking in the abstract actually before him, and knows that it is he, and can say to himself, 'This is the man or this is the character who ought to have a certain argument applied to him in order to convince him of a certain opinion';—he who knows all this, and knows also when he should speak and when he should refrain, and when he should use pithy sayings, pathetic appeals, sensational affects, and all the other modes of speech which he has learned;—when, I say, he knows the times and seasons of all these things, then, and not till then, he is a perfect master of his art; but if he fail in any of these points, whether in speaking or teaching or writing them, and yet declares that he speaks by rules of art, he who says 'I don't believe you' has the better of him.

—Plato, *Phaedrus*, 272

Chapter 5

GUILT-EDGED BONDS: THE CLIMATE OF DECISION

THE SMITH broadcasts did not affect all listeners in the same fashion. Some listened continuously with mounting interest and others, quite unmoved by her appeals, soon turned to other pursuits. Some purchased bonds and others did not. Nor is there any assurance that all those who bought bonds were actuated by the same aspects of her broadcasts. In short, we have yet to explore the differential effects of the Smith marathon upon different types of listeners.

Decisions induced by persuasion may be regarded as the resultant of three interrelated variables. First and most apparent of these is the structure and content of the persuasive arguments. Plainly, different appeals, variously presented, will evoke different responses and lead to different decisions. The second variable is the nature of the affective relationship between the person advancing the arguments and the person responding to them.[1] The same lines of argument will often meet with quite varied responses according to whether they are put forward by those toward whom one feels sympathetic or antagonistic. And the third of these variables is comprised by the predispositions of the persons subjected to the persuasive appeals. In analyzing the decisions to buy or not to buy a war bond, we must consider the relations between the content of

---

[1] Muzafer Sherif reviews some of the experimental evidence establishing the significance of this variable. *The Psychology of Social Norms* (New. York: Harpers, 1936), pp. 120 ff.

Smith's appeals, listeners' attitudes toward Smith and their pre-dispositions.

We can anticipate that these decisions resulted from different patterns of motivation. Not all those who bought a war bond from Smith were persuaded by the same elements of the broadcast, nor were they influenced to the same degree. So, too, different predispositions induced responses to diverse features of the total situation. In one pattern, it was the relation to Smith that provided the major motivation; in another a sense of guilt, reinforced to the point where it could no longer be tolerated. But such variations did not occur at random.

In this chapter, we shall examine the various clusters of motives in the light of varying predispositions among those 75 buyers of bonds from Smith who were interviewed at length.

Listeners' Predispositions

Whatever their ultimate sources, the predispositions of listeners directly pertinent to the Smith bond drive were compounded of two attitudes. The first is a basic, continuing orientation toward war bonds and their significance, built up over a period of five years in which Americans had been exposed to an insistent emphasis on the place of war bonds in a national emergency. Comparatively stable and enduring, this *"general orientation"* toward war bonds is quite distinct from the second component of predispositions: the *"specific attitude"* toward the purchase of additional bonds during the Third War Loan drive. Whatever their general orientation, some listeners had definitely planned to buy additional bonds, others had decided not to do so. Obviously, the susceptibility to Smith's appeals would vary according to the listener's state of readiness to add to his stock of war bonds during this drive.

These two components, then—general orientation and specific attitude—are taken to comprise the predispositions of listeners.

General Orientations. To be sure, the general attitude toward war bonds probably was favorable among the vast majority of Americans at the time of the drive. Only one of our informants—an acidulous ex-count who had known better days in Imperial Russia—expressed a hostile attitude toward war bonds, insisting in a veritable cataract of indignation that "I wouldn't buy them at any price. I would consider buying a bond as burned money, because I know I'll never get it back, and I resent that the government is lying to me, that I will get it back, to feel fooled that the government is promising things that they will never live up to."

But despite the general approval of war bonds, there were variations in the intensity of emotional involvement with bonds as a symbol, as an instrumentality for helping to bring the war to a close and as a moral obligation. General orientations ranged from the pole of deep emotional involvement to that of mild, almost detached approval. At the one extreme were those who, whatever the extent of their contributions, felt a profound sense of guilt over the insufficiency of what they had done and who made considerable sacrifices to buy war bonds. "It would make me feel rotten not to get a bond, because I feel I ought to buy. I've got to do it; there can't be any excuse not to. We're in the war; we've got to win and we need the money to win. And the quicker we get the boys back, we won't have that awful strain on our minds." "I live on nine dollars a week and what's left over from the allotment I get from my son overseas goes into bonds and bonds only. I wish I could buy more and get this mess over with." Sixty-three of the seventy-five informants who bought a war bond from Smith exhibited such emotional involvement, whereas the remaining twelve were comparatively "detached" in their general orientations.

These latter are the people who merely repeated favorable clichés about the significance of bonds or who regarded war bonds primarily as a secure investment. "I buy bonds because they are a good way to tie up useless funds."

It might be assumed that people with moderate or high incomes would feel more strongly obligated to buy war bonds than those with low incomes. In our sample of informants, at least, this did not prove to be the case. In both upper and lower income strata, the usual reason for not feeling deeply obligated held that "we're buying all we can afford." And in most of these cases, high and low income alike,

General Orientation toward War Bonds of Two Income Strata			
Income Strata	Involved	Detached	No.
	%	%	..
Upper	75	25	39
Lower	84	16	61

"all we can afford" was defined as approximately 10 per cent of income. This appears to have been a standardized definition common to the several income levels, yet it is clear from our interviews that abiding by this standard meant entirely different things on various income levels. We found, for example, a low-income family sacrificing the money they had put aside for a much-needed layette, whereas on the high-income level bond purchases merely involved the transfer of funds from a savings account or the decision not to buy an extra fur coat. So, too, among non-buyers, there were unmarried high-income people who felt no further obligation to pledge a bond since they had bought their accustomed 10 per cent, and low-income people with large families, apparently converting into bonds all that was available beyond the bare necessities, who exhibited no strong feeling of further obligation because they too were buying "all we can afford."

Why the virtual complacency about the 10 per cent standard? Basically, of course, it derived from the fact that this had been publicized as the expected level of war bond investment.

A standard had been socially established and it seemed "right." Had a differential standard graduated with income been proposed, that, too, would probably have been accepted and regarded as a reasonable obligation. The proportion one could afford for wartime "sacrifices" was an indeterminate matter in which the individual had no clear basis for reaching an independent judgment and in which, therefore, one relied on an established social norm.[2] In such an ambiguous situation, once a social standard had been set forth, it was regarded as a legitimate measure of each individual's conduct.

The constant proportional norm may nonetheless have a substantial basis rooted in the social psychology of our society. The economist, Harold F. Clark, discovered in a study some years ago that, whatever people's normal income might be, each person thought that about 25 per cent additional income would be enough to eliminate anxiety and strain and provide a comfortable sense of security. This proportion was constant on low as well as high income levels. In the same way, it appears that 10 per cent of income invested in war bonds came to be considered about what each can afford, regardless of the size of the base on which it was computed. For the most part, conformity with the norm largely eliminated self-accusations about not contributing sufficiently to the over-all war effort, although it will become evident that, under special circumstances, an intensely emotional general orientation toward war bonds led to a change in this norm.

Specific Attitudes. On the day of the Smith marathon, not only general orientations but also the specific attitudes of listeners varied between two extremes. Listeners had either a well-defined intention to buy more bonds in the course of the drive or, for various reasons, no intention of doing so. Of course, both the definiteness and the intensity of this attitudinal

2 See the general statement of this pattern in Sherif, *op. cit.*

set varied among our informants but, by and large, they could be grouped into these two categories. Such specific predispositions among persons who eventually did buy a bond from Smith were more evenly distributed than were the general orientations: 43 had a definite intent to purchase more bonds and 31 had no intention of doing so. (One bond buyer could not be classified in this regard.)

By combining these two elements of general orientation and specific attitude, we obtain four types of predispositions, as set forth in the following list which also indicates the number of bond buyers in each of these groups:

Purchaser's Predisposition toward War Bonds		No. of
General Orientation	Specific Attitude	Cases
1. *Predisposed:* emotionally involved and	intended to buy extra bonds	35
2. *Susceptible:* emotionally involved and	did not intend to buy extra bonds	28
3. *Indifferent:* detached	and intended to buy extra bonds	8
4. *Undisposed:* detached	and did not intend to buy extra bonds	3
	Total	74

Plainly, we should expect persons in these four groups to be variously vulnerable to appeals for the purchase of war bonds. They should have varying degrees of resistance. Those with favorable general orientations and with specific intent to buy additional bonds clearly have the lowest level of resistance; indeed, they may properly be termed the "predisposed" group. At the other extreme, those who are apathetic with respect to bonds and who, for whatever reasons, did not intend to buy more during the drive, exhibit the highest level of resistance and may appropriately be described as "undisposed." The intermediate groups have a favorable predisposition either in general orientation or in specific attitude, and are termed "susceptible" and "indifferent," respectively. Varying as they did, each of these groups presented different problems of persuasion.

Just how did persuasion operate in these four groups of bond buyers? To deal with this question, we shall keep one variable constant—the predisposition—and examine the workings of the two other variables in persuasion: the content of the appeals and the relations of listeners to the person making the appeals. In other words, rather than assume that the Smith war bond drive affected all buyers in precisely the same fashion, we shall systematically explore the processes of persuasion for those who were in different states of readiness to buy bonds at the time they first heard the Smith broadcasts. In this way, through analysis of the interview materials, we shall be able to discern the patterns of motivation which actuated decisions to buy a war bond from Smith, although the paucity of cases makes the interpretation suggestive rather than conclusive.

The Smith Appeals as Catalyst: The Predisposed Bond Buyer

Every effort at mass persuasion must deal with an audience the members of which vary to some extent in their readiness to respond. As their dispositions vary, so do their levels of resistance to persuasion and their selective responses to various phases of the stimulus field. Thus, during the Smith bond drive, we should expect this resistance to be least among the predisposed listeners: those persons who attached great emotional significance to war bonds and who had made a prior decision to buy additional bonds during the drive, having earmarked funds for this purpose. This was the group of the preconverted, so to speak. The task confronting Smith in obtaining bond pledges from this sector of the audience was not to convince them of the singular importance of war bonds or to induce them to buy additional bonds, but only to persuade them to buy their bonds at once and to buy them from her.

Several types of evidence testify to the comparatively slight degree of persuasion that was exercised among the predisposed listeners. As we should expect if our classification of predispositions is valid, the predisposed group listened to fewer of Smith's broadcasts before making their decision to pledge a bond to her than did those with higher levels of resistance. A slight prod proved sufficient. They heard an average of 12 broadcasts, in comparison with an average of 16 for the "susceptible" group (i.e., those who had a favorable general orientation but did not intend to buy extra bonds). Further data point to the same conclusion. Whereas 25 per cent of those in the three other predisposition groups heard more than 20 broadcasts before reaching their decision, only 15 per cent of the predisposed group heard that many appeals, and these had actually arrived at a decision early in the series, but had been unable to telephone their pledge earlier because of extraneous obstacles: "I decided the very first time, but something was wrong with the telephone, and it was taken to the superintendent's office to be fixed." And again: "I couldn't call her until 11 at night, when I closed the store."

These facts merely confirm our hypothesis that different *degrees* of persuasion were required for listeners with varying predispositions. We have yet to consider the *patterns* of persuasion among the several predisposition groups. A pertinent clue is suggested by several psychological theories, which agree on one central theorem: the aspects of a stimulus field which are perceived and responded to are largely determined by the attitudinal set.[3] Hungry and satiated persons will respond dif-

[3] This is not the place to review the extensive experimental and theoretical materials which support this hypothesis. We need note only that a variety of "schools" of psychology and sociology converge on this view. Gestalt psychology, psychoanalysis, field theory, the "sociology of knowledge," for example, all seek to incorporate this fact into their theory. Early experiments on the role of *Aufgaben* (tasks or problems), stemming from Külpe, found that the aspects most clearly perceived in a stimulus field were largely determined by the nature of the problem set the subjects. The concept of "perspectives" in the sociology of knowledge refers to the tendency to perceive the external world in terms of a socially determined outlook. For a partial review of this material, see Sherif, *op. cit.*, Chapter 3.

ferently to the promise of food; anxiety-ridden and secure persons will react differently to rumors of war; persons who have made a prior decision to buy war bonds should respond to different aspects of bond propaganda than those who had no such intent.

Since the predisposed group had been previously convinced of the high significance of war bonds and had made a prior decision to buy additional bonds, they would not be expected to attend markedly to those phases of the Smith broadcasts which advocated these ideas. All this constituted a closed chapter for them. Instead, they would be expected to single out and respond to those aspects of the situation which were still unsettled, namely, the bases for buying a bond at once and for buying it from Smith.

The interview data for the predisposed listeners fully bear out these theoretical expectations. They paid comparatively little attention to the content of Smith's appeals which emphasized the patriotic and affective significance of bonds. Only 31 per cent of the *predisposed* bond buyers, compared with 61 per cent of the *susceptible* group (with no prior intent to buy) indicated a marked concern with the *content* of Smith's appeals.[4] These were the persons who "listened with only one ear," who frequently reported that they "don't remember what she said." It is as though, set to buy as they were, it was enough to learn that this presented another occasion for the purchase of bonds.

In similar fashion, the predisposed listeners were largely unconcerned with the endurance and "sacrifice" aspects of Smith's drive. "I was buying the bond anyway, so I had no

---

[4] All interviews were subjected to a thorough content analysis on the basis of which they were classified in terms of the degree of interest expressed in the emotional content of the Smith appeals. These results are particularly suggestive, inasmuch as this classification was originally made without the present hypothesis in view.

special reaction to her." They were less likely to respond to this dimension of the total situation. Only 34 per cent of them, as compared with 54 per cent of the susceptible group, regarded her effort as an exalted achievement. The selective character of the persuasion experience is indicated even more clearly by judgments of the two groups of listeners on the amount of physical and emotional strain under which Smith was laboring. The predisposed buyers less often sympathized and empathized with the presumably valiant efforts of Smith during the marathon. Only 17 per cent of the predisposed listeners in contrast to 52 per cent of the susceptible group expressed the conviction that she exhibited signs of great strain.

From all this, it appears that the predisposed group largely ignored those aspects of the Smith propaganda designed to provide general motivation for the purchase of war bonds. Instead, they focused primarily upon those elements in the Smith broadcasts which were *pertinent for the only elements of their decision still unresolved:* should we purchase our bonds at this time or later and should we purchase our bonds from Smith?

But even this limited assignment in persuasion required the overcoming of some resistance. The prior dispositions to buy bonds ranged from an intention to make the purchase "at some time" during the drive to a definite commitment to buy from a specific person or organization. And these variations in disposition posed two distinct problems in persuasion. For the first group of predisposed listeners, Smith had merely to *canalize* their intention to purchase the bonds then and there; for the second, she had to *displace* their intention to buy from others. Correlatively, each of these groups of listeners tended to focus on distinctive aspects of Smith's appeals.

For 18 of the predisposed listeners, the occasion primarily provided a bridge from their prior decision to the immediate action. "I was going to buy one anyway; it was a reminder." It is impossible to determine, of course, whether all those with a stated intention to purchase a bond would have done so, had they not been exposed to the Smith broadcasts. Her drive was perceived as an immediate and convenient opportunity for removing any lingering doubts. "I had planned to buy one anyway, but Kate Smith gave me a push." It enabled some to convert an intention into a commitment: "I decided to call even though I did not have the money in the house, *so that I would have it in. I wanted to be sure I had it ordered, that's why I called.*" Similarly, others recognized that as long as they deferred the actual purchase, their good intentions were subject to the attrition of competing claims and expenditures. As one housewife put it, "the money would have been harder to part with the longer I waited." For these, the Smith drive afforded a ready occasion for resolving a conflict.

The remaining 17 of the predisposed group had planned to buy their extra bonds from a specific person or agency. In all but three of these cases, the "persuasion" by Smith represented not a genuine increase in the total amount of war bonds sold in the national drive but merely a transfer from one source to another. These three persons had been persuaded in advance, so to speak, since they had deliberately waited for the Smith drive in order to purchase their bonds from her. The others represent clear instances of displacement. In all likelihood, if they had not heard Smith's broadcast, they would have carried out their original plans.

The necessity of displacing their intention to purchase bonds from another source would seem to have set Smith a peculiarly difficult problem in persuasion. Actually, there was no great problem here of countering other obligations or loyalties, for, without exception, these predisposed listeners had planned to make their purchase from an impersonal agency, such as a bank or post office. No significant personal commitment was involved. Some preferred to purchase their bond from a person whom "they knew" rather than from an agency with which they had no personal relationship. "Why should I go some place I don't know when I can go some place I do? *I feel I know Kate.*"

And, in point of fact, there is corroborative evidence that a sense of close personal relationship with Smith was more likely to play a role among those predisposed buyers whose prior intentions were *displaced* than among those whose intentions were merely *canalized*. Thus, 3 of every 4 of the "displaced" group as compared with 1 of every 3 of the "canalized" group had a warm personal attachment for Smith. Since their prior intent to purchase from another source was not rooted in sentiment, the change in decision did not entail any emotional conflict. Against the background of a favorable attitude toward Smith, predisposed listeners seized upon the comparative ease of telephoning a pledge as the basis for their decision. "I thought it would be much easier by phone; you just send back the application with the money order." "I didn't want to wait in line."

In sum, this group of predisposed bond buyers required relatively little persuasion, having previously made the decision to add to their stock of bonds and having set aside funds to this end. They were poised for persuasion. This attitudinal set so patterned their responses that they attended to some and largely ignored other dimensions of the Smith broadcasts. Their pattern of selective response, organized in terms of those features of the total bond-buying situation which still involved unrelieved tensions, is preliminary evidence of the inadequacy of any general statement that "the" Smith appeals proved effective. For these persons, attention was skewed in the direction of those aspects of the total situation pertinent for those phases of their decision which were not yet fully structured:

when and where to make their purchase. As a consequence, the "irrelevant" content of Smith's appeals—the patriotic and affective significance of bonds, the sacrifice of fighting men and civilians, etc.—was not the object of attention. Instead, the dimensions of listener's affective relationships with Smith and, above all, the sheer convenience of buying their preappointed bond—"just telephone your pledge"—took the foreground of attention. Smith activated the general orientation of these listeners toward war bonds. This pattern of response differs in most salient respects from that characteristic of the "susceptible" group of bond buyers who, despite their emotional conviction of the importance of war bonds, did not intend to purchase any more bonds during the Third War Loan drive.

Guilt and Decision: The Susceptible Bond Buyer

Before exposure to the Smith broadcasts, the 28 informants in the "susceptible" group felt that they had discharged their bond obligations. Eleven had previously met their self-set quota of bonds during the drive and the others felt "we are doing all we can with payroll deductions." Since their prior purchases satisfied their established standards, they had reached a temporary equilibrium in which their ego level could be preserved intact. "I had bought bonds in the community the week before, and felt that was all I needed to buy." "I wasn't going to buy a bond, because we've already bought *our bonds.*" "I usually buy bonds through the bank. I thought I'd let it slip for a couple of months; *I was ahead of my pledge.*" "We always buy our bonds the first day of the drive. *We had already bought our share when I heard her.*" Smith led these listeners to reassess the adequacy of their previous contributions. She disturbed the previously stabilized ego level by inviting a series of reappraisals of the implicit standards in terms of which a sense of adequacy had been attained. How did this come about?

As we have seen, a larger proportion of the susceptible buyers responded to all the persuasive elements of the broadcast: more were greatly devoted to Smith, more were impressed by the extent of her effort, and more were acutely interested in the content of her appeals. Furthermore, only four of the 28 had funds readily available for the purchase, in contrast to the predisposed who had, of course, specifically set aside their money for this purpose. And since they had a higher level of resistance, they listened to more appeals before deciding to pledge a bond (1 of every 4 heard Smith 20 times or more before coming to a decision).

It is significant that, in contrast to the predisposed group who characteristically explained their decision as a matter of convenience, the susceptible group phrased their "motivation" in terms of a renewed sense of guilt. Various aspects of the Smith broadcasts served to redefine the appropriate amount of bonds to be purchased and, in the light of these modified norms, an acute sense of unworthiness and self-accusation intervened. Without implying that a single factor in the total situation initiated this process of self-revaluation, we can conveniently classify the susceptible listeners in three categories, according to the aspects of the broadcasts to which they chiefly responded.[5] Some repeatedly stressed the magnitude of Smith's effort and described in circumstantial detail how this led them to re-examine their own contributions to the war effort. Others phrased the basis for their behavior chiefly in terms of their affective relationship to Smith. And still others were primarily influenced by the accounts of sacrifice by soldiers which led to an upward revision of norms for their own conduct.

[5] At the risk of undue repetition, it should be emphasized that we do not thereby subscribe to the view that action results from isolated impulses or motives. We are here analyzing our informants' own phrasing of the aspects which led to a reconsideration of their previous decision not to buy additional bonds during the drive.

As the day wore on, listeners in the first category were increasingly affected by Smith's "self-sacrifice." In the context of her seemingly extreme and selfless effort, their own earlier contributions fell short. They were no longer convinced that they had done enough: "By evening, she was still going so strong. I admired her endurance. *I felt if she had made such an effort, why shouldn't I make another bit of an effort?*"

The Phrasing of Motivation among Susceptible Bond Buyers

	No. of Cases
Smith's "sacrifice" (the marathon)	16
Affective relationship (devotion to Smith)	5
Content of Smith appeals (others' sacrifices)	6
Unclassified	1
Total	28

The recurring theme throughout these sixteen interviews is expressed in the following excerpts:

"I'd already bought one for the drive. Then I began to feel I should have done a little more than I had . . . *She was doing her bit to help the boys carry on.* I would have felt uneasy . . . I don't know . . . if I hadn't bought."

"*If she could stay on the radio all day like that, the least I could do was to buy another bond.* I wouldn't feel right listening all day and then going into a bank and not buying from her. *Maybe if she were only on for an hour or two, like the others, it wouldn't matter.*"

Following the bond purchase, these listeners experienced a release of tension, as though they had again satisfied legitimate demands which had been laid upon them. They had regained their self-regard.

"After I bought, I could sleep—before that I couldn't close my eyes. It was almost one o'clock by the time I bought the bond. I thought, '*poor darling, she certainly earned that thirty million she sold.' At one o'clock, I said, 'Now that I've done my little job, I thank God for giving me the wisdom to see clearly,' and I turned off the radio.*"

For these persons, then, it was not what Smith said that day that prompted the purchase, but what she did. Accounts of the sacrifices of fighting men did not move them to self-reappraisal. They had previously bought sufficient bonds to alleviate any guilt feelings evoked by these more familiar themes. For them, the reappraisal came about through a more direct, forceful, and new impact—provided, in this instance, by Smith's personal example.

Among the five buyers who bought bonds primarily as a testimonial to their long-standing devotion to Smith, there was little activation of guilt. This is evidenced by their tendency to lose sight of the fact that they were buying *bonds*, rather than answering a request by Smith. Their beloved Kate was making an appeal, and they gave to *her*. Had she been asking for clothing for the worthy poor, books for the bedridden, or toys for deprived children, their response would probably have been the same: "*She asked for something*, and I gave it to her." "I bought as soon as I knew she wanted it. . . . *If I like Kate Smith so much, I have to prove it.*" "I said to myself, No, Kate, I won't let you down on this." These pledges, then, did not stem from a reorientation toward war bonds or a revision of personal norms of bond purchases. In a sense, they did not so much represent war bond pledges as pledges of personal attachment to Smith.[6]

For the remaining six persons among the susceptible buyers,

[6] A similar pattern has been found in the field of political behavior. ". . . personal influence, with all its overtones of personal affection and loyalty, can bring to the polls votes that would otherwise not be cast or would be cast for the opposing party just as readily if some other friend had insisted . . . Fully 25% of those who mentioned a personal contact in connection with change of mind failed to give a real issue of the campaign as a reason for the change, but only 5% of those who mentioned the formal media. omitted such a reason. When personal influence is paramount in this way, the voter is voting mainly for the personal friend, not the candidate." P. F. Lazarsfeld, B. Berelson and H. Gaudet, *The People's Choice* (New York: Duell, Sloan & Pearce, 1944), p. 157.

the process of persuasion was phrased in considerably different terms. They revised their bond obligations upward in response to the content of Smith's appeals. Closer examination of these six cases indicates that they were especially vulnerable to one of these appeals and for a particular reason.

We have noted that a central theme in the Smith broadcasts could be summarized in these terms: Buy a bond and bring your boy back home. And it was to this theme that these persons chiefly responded. A series of interlocking data indicate that the context of this selective response was provided by their deep personal involvement in the war. To begin with, four of the listeners in this category were mothers of sons in the armed forces; the fifth had a brother in the service, and the sixth was himself a veteran of the first World War. In contrast, only 9 of the 22 others in the susceptible category had close relatives (son, brother, husband or father) in some branch of the service.

Further data account for this selective response. These five persons were peculiarly beset by fears and anxiety

Responded to Accounts of Soldier Sacrifice	Close Relatives in Armed Forces		
	Yes	No	Total
Yes	5	1	6
No	9	13	22
Total	14	14	28

concerning a son or brother who, in all five instances, was serving overseas. They were, therefore, peculiarly sensitive to Smith's vivid portrayals of the needs and sacrifices of men at the front. It was as though they visualized their own sons as the central figures in the dramatic episodes described by Smith. Phrases which were little more than clichés for others took on deep emotional significance for those who interpreted them in the light of their own longings and anxieties. Thus, almost echoing a Smith phrase, one informant in this category defined her bond purchase as a means of "bringing my brother home sooner."

Within this context of emotional stress, Smith's appeals were taken by mothers as presenting a means of coping with the apprehensions that crowded in upon them. They felt themselves at the mercy of incalculable circumstances. There was the ever-present imminence of fateful word from the War Department—We regret to inform you . . . Faced with these obsessive fears, it was psychologically difficult for them to arrive at the dispassionate judgment that nothing could be done to enhance the safety of their sons. All this generated a powerful need for "doing something" about an unendurable situation and, under the goad of this desperate anxiety, the bond purchase took on an almost magical character.[7] For, tormented by terrible forebodings, these mothers acted as though the *particular* bond they bought would directly safeguard their own sons in battle, as though *their* bonds would set in motion circumstances which would bring their boys safe through the war. *Something* was being done, and the sense of helplessness and lack of control over an unbearable, ego-charged danger gave way to a feeling of having introduced some measure of control.[8] Smith's vivid accounts of the horrors to which fighting

[7] Compare Malinowski's account of "the type of situation in which we find magic." "Man, engaged in a series of practical activities, *comes to a gap;* the hunter is disappointed in his quarry, the sailor misses propitious winds, the canoe-builder has to deal with some material of which he is never certain that it will stand the strain, or the healthy person suddenly feels his strength failing. What does man do naturally under such conditions, setting aside all magic, belief and ritual? Forsaken by his knowledge, baffled by his past experience and by his technical skill, *he realises his impotence. Yet his desire grips him only the more strongly; his anxiety, his fears and hopes, induce a tension in his organism which drives him to some sort of activity.* Whether he be savage or civilised, whether in possession of magic or entirely ignorant of its existence, *passive inaction*, the only thing dictated by reason, *is the last thing in which he can acquiesce.* His nervous system and his whole organism drive him to some *substitute activity.*" B. Malinowski, "Magic, Science and Religion," in *Science, Religion and Reality* (ed. by Joseph Needham) (New York: The Macmillan Company, 1925, p. 73). (Italics inserted.)

[8] "The function of magic is to ritualise man's optimism, to enhance his faith in the victory of hope over fear." *Ibid.*, p. 83.

men are exposed thus had a double-edged character: they virtually terrorized these mothers into an added bond purchase and by doing so, provided a behavior formula for temporary escape from intolerable fears and anxieties.

Translating Smith's appeals into acutely personal terms, the anxious mother of a bombardier stationed in England felt that her bond was to serve as direct aid to her son.

"I remember she say, 'If you buy a bond, you buy a ticket for your son to come home.' [At this point, the interviewer was shown a photograph of her son.] She was just like speaking to me. Her voice . . . she helps mothers, our sons, I cried all the time. [She asks the interviewer: You think maybe our boys come home soon?] The way she speaks to mothers, it would break anyone's heart. I think: I am going to buy a bond. *I'll buy a bond for my boy. I wouldn't NOT have the money to help my son. I wouldn't be able to rest.*"

A Brooklyn housewife, whose only son was overseas, similarly supplied a personal context for Smith's accounts of sacrifice, as the following excerpt indicates:

"The way she was talking, I had all I could do to get to the phone quickly. She was telling the story of a young fellow— I remember his name, Merrill—that didn't have any legs or arms and was happy and wanted no sympathy and that we should buy bonds in his name *and save some other boy from such a thing. It touched very deeply. Not only what she said. But my son's in the service for three years* . . . It got me so. I ran from the phone right over to his picture and started to cry. And I said: '*Sonny, if this will save one hair on your head,* I thank God, and I thank God that I live in the United States.'"

In those instances where mothers had no knowledge of their sons' whereabouts or of the risks to which they were exposed, anxieties were all the more intensified. The absence of any secure basis for judgment gave free rein to all manner of apprehensions which they sought to escape by actively doing something for their boys:

> "I tell you, I was pretty well upset. I sent my daughter to call her up. *I hadn't heard from my boy for some time and I was worried.* [Informant gives way to tears.] It's funny how some people don't give. It's only a loan. If I had more money, I'd given it all. [Informant finds it increasingly difficult to speak.] I feel foolish, but I can't help myself. I'm so upset about my son on the Flying Fortress. *Every time she spoke, it meant more and more. I was so upset. It made me wish I could have given her all—everything I had to give up for the boy.* I was trying to get some money together to get curtains, but I put up with the old ones."

> "I was listening to Kate's stories and started to think of my son. He trained in the Seventh Regiment. It was just that she was asking for money and my boy is in the war. *I don't even know where he is now. His A.P.O. number has been changed.*"

But all this does not explain why only 5 of the 14 listeners with close relatives in the armed forces responded in this fashion. What of the "deviate" cases, those 9 who did *not* respond selectively to this phase of Smith's appeals? An analysis of the interviews provides the clue. The unresponsive persons had little basis for acute fears or anxiety concerning the safety of sons or brothers in the service. In five cases, their kin were stationed in this country and, therefore, their situation did not evoke immediate anxiety. And in another instance, where a son was overseas, he was far removed from any active war theater. Nor could a chief gunner's mate, the husband of another informant, be a source of anxiety, since at the time he was home on leave and listening with his wife to the Smith bond drive. Thus, the emotional context for selective listening was significantly different for the two categories of informants, although both had close relatives in the Army or Navy.

In review, then, the evidence suggests that susceptible listeners responded selectively in terms of distinctive sets of determinants. By taking "close relatives in the service" as a crude index of direct emotional involvement with the war, we found a tendency for those who were emotionally involved to respond particularly to the "sacrifice" theme of Smith's broadcasts. But this led to the problem of interpreting the absence of such selective response among some relatives of servicemen. A further refinement of our index in terms of those relationships which did or did not generate anxiety enabled us to account for such seeming "exceptions." It was against the background of acute anxiety concerning the safety of affectively significant persons in the armed services that some informants were particularly affected by the sacrificial theme.

This pattern suggests the apparent paradox that those who had already contributed most heavily to the national war effort—by giving a son or brother to the service and by previous bond purchases—were perhaps the most likely to continue giving more. Their initial emotional involvement provided the motivational basis for further cumulative contributions, whereas those who had a less immediate, a psychologically less compelling stake in the war were not as likely to have the same urgent drive for all-out sacrifice. Each successive emotional commitment induced further commitment, if only because it made for successive gratifications.[9] We do not know, of course, the frequency of *this pattern of cumulative and self-reinforcing response*[10] in the general population, but its occur-

[9] The previously quoted mother of a crew member of a Flying Fortress provides a case in point: "I've given my blood to the Red Cross five times and I plan to go again soon . . ."

[10] A similar pattern has been exhibited in other contexts. It is found in the "self-selection of audiences," so that, for example, opinion-shaping radio programs have audiences comprised in the main of persons in full agreement with the views being broadcast. Mass meetings centered about a *cause célèbre* ordinarily attract those who have the "appropriate" attitudes at the outset and thus produce reinforcement rather than diffusion of atti-

rence among our informants suggests the possibility that the main weight of contributions to the war effort may be borne, for understandable psychological reasons, by particular sectors of the nation.[11]

Detachment and Decision

As we have seen, eleven informants who bought a bond from Smith exhibited a comparatively unemotional, detached orientation toward war bonds. Eight of these—the "indifferent"—had planned to buy additional bonds during the drive and three —the "undisposed"—had no such intention. These are the persons who prevailingly regard war bonds as a "practical investment," rather than a patriotic symbol or an essential instrumentality in the war effort.

"I think the investment part, the saving part, is important. If the country fails, our money won't be any good anyway. If we win, we get it back."

"It's just for a rainy day. I think that's a pretty logical reason. Ten years from today, we don't know what straits we'll be in and then the money may come in handy. I don't want to cash in any of them. You know what I'd really like to do? If I could, I'd like to buy enough to take care of my son's education."

The paucity of cases in the two groups of "detached" buyers does not permit us to establish comparative patterns of per-

tudes. The effects tend to be cumulative rather than dispersive. Cf. P. F. Lazarsfeld "The Effects of Radio on Public Opinion," *Print, Radio and Film in a Democracy* (Douglas Waples, ed.) (University of Chicago Press, 1942), pp. 68–69.

[11] This may be mitigated by a countertendency on the part of guilt-ridden persons to "compensate" for their seemingly inadequate contributions to a common cause. The veteran who responded to the "sacrifice theme" illustrates this pattern: "I never gave buying a bond a thought before I heard her. The stories she told of the suffering of the boys on the other side comes right back to you. The last one she was telling got me. It reminded me of something that happened twenty-five years ago on the other side. And it made me want to buy. *At least I can buy bonds. I can't do anything else.*"

suasion, but these few instances do provide a basis for interpretions which have some measure of plausibility. We can readily understand, for example, why the eight indifferent listeners who were poised for a bond purchase listened to an average of only eight broadcasts, fewer than that of any other predisposition group. In contrast to the predisposed group, they had little affective or emotional concern with war bonds, and in contrast to those who had no prior intent to buy a bond, they required little cumulative persuasion. Their decision was quickly made, and there was little further motivation for continued listening.

In accord with their prevalently utilitarian attitude toward bonds, their decision to purchase their bond from Smith rather than from others stemmed largely from promised gratifications which had little or no relation to bonds as a focus of sentiment. Thus the prospect of a personal, even though ephemeral, contact with a celebrity played a conspicuous role in their decision. Five of the eight persons in this category telephoned their pledge

Predisposition Category	Expectation of Smith Personally Answering Telephone Pledge		
	+	−	Total
Indifferent	5	3	8
All other buyers	12	55	67
Total	17	58	75

in the hope of speaking personally to Smith, whereas only 12 of the 55 other bond buyers were actuated by this consideration. The decision to buy was less a matter of purchasing a sentiment-laden bond than an occasion for direct personal contact with a prestigeful public figure. This motive was typically expressed by an informant who, to say the least, was otherwise atypical—she is an attendant to a "half-woman, half-serpent freak" in a mid-Manhattan "museum":

"Reptilina and I sat talking about it for a few minutes first. [At this point, the articulate Reptilina herself interrupted to explain: *"We thought about calling because we would be able to talk to Kate herself."*] Then I said, well, I'll call up. I did, and found out that Kate was not talking to people. She really couldn't, now that I think of it, because so many people called up. But I couldn't back out then. I would have felt like a fool. Besides, I was going to buy one anyway."

Another basis for the decision, extraneous to any emotional meaning ascribed to bonds, is found in their affective ties to Smith. In seven cases, they were devoted fans who readily sought this new opportunity of expressing their sentiment. "Being an admirer of hers, I just called." The present experience occurred within the context of previous sentimental attachments to Smith, ties imbued with considerable affect. Thus, when one such listener heard the bond broadcasts, she was flooded with nostalgic images of what Smith had meant to her in the past:

> "About eleven or twelve years ago, I was very ill. I was sitting all alone. It was wintertime. The ground was all white with snow, the trees and everything. And nothing could be more realistic than Kate singing, 'When the Moon Comes Over the Mountain'. . . . Thoughts came quickly back to me of that night when I was down in spirit and health, too. It's something I don't think anything can express. I was anxious to see her do well. . . . *I think there's a natural desire where anyone you've contacted* . . . [and, then, as the actual character of the 'personal' tie is half-recognized] . . . *maybe, not personally. She had set her goal and I wanted to help her meet it."*

And, finally, since all these persons had planned to purchase their bonds at a post office or bank, they were not at all subjected to a conflict of personal loyalties.

This configuration of factors—detached attitude, immediate intent to purchase, comparatively slight attention devoted to the broadcasts, and primary concern with relationship to Smith

—reduced the likelihood of any focus on the content of Smith's appeals. There is little evidence of any marked response to the themes of her broadcast among the "indifferent" bond buyers. And, in consequence, there were no signs that these listeners experienced a reorientation toward their secular conception of war bonds. In large measure, Smith simply provided another, seemingly convenient occasion for the planned bond purchase and, in these instances at least, left unmodified the previous detached attitudes toward war bonds.

Among the "undisposed" listeners, i.e., those who had a detached orientation toward war bonds and had no prior intent to buy a bond, the major element in persuasion was clearly their close affective tie to Smith. This becomes evident from a comparison between the three undisposed persons who finally pledged a bond to Smith and the six who were not persuaded to do so. We have seen that comparatively few persons in our sample expressed an unfavorable attitude toward Smith (only 18 per cent of our informants). But all six of the undisposed nonbuyers fall in this category, whereas all three who purchased a bond had positive feelings toward her.

This positive sentiment in turn resulted in readiness to continue listening to her broadcasts. Two listened to the radio considerably more than usual (one by-passing favorite programs on other stations for this purpose) and the third maintained her customary degree of listening. "I didn't even turn the radio off after I went to bed." Among the nonbuyers, on the other hand, there was a distinct avoidance of the Smith broadcasts, as a consequence of their pre-existing attitudes. "I listened less. I made a point not to listen the rest of the evening." "I turned on something else and she butted in . . . I didn't pay any attention to her." Among the undisposed buyers, then, a strong tie to Smith induced continued listening and thus provided an *opportunity* for responding to the themes of the broadcasts, whereas the undisposed nonbuyers largely shut themselves off from this influence through "self-selection."

Since the sentiment that governed their behavior centered in Smith rather than in war bonds, the undisposed buyers proved more sensitive to the "sacrifice" of Smith herself than to that of the unknown persons to whom she referred. Invariably, their reports of self-reappraisal induced by the broadcasts are focused on Smith: "*She* was doing so much. I felt she ought to get all the response possible, so I added my bit . . ." "*She* deserved a big result . . . My feelings were she was overexerting herself."

The same major orientation toward Smith is manifested in their reactions to the accounts of the sacrifices of "our boys." The accent is primarily on Smith's presentation of these episodes rather than on their actual content:

> "*The way she was pleading*—it was for her own children. A mother couldn't have pleaded more. I don't know how anyone could resist. I visualized her taking a nap, exhausted, her voice was trembling."

> "*She was so earnest and appealing.* I don't know a thing she said. *It was the way she talked. I couldn't tell you a story she told*, but her general way of talking and putting things across . . ."

And, finally, all three informants had easy access to funds. They experienced no great obstacle to translating their devotion to Smith into an appropriate act. The prototype of sacrifice by an authoritative figure whom they loved invited a fresh decision and culminated in the tension-relieving purchase of a bond:

> "After listening about twenty-two times, I jumped up from the chair when I decided I couldn't stand it. I couldn't listen to her anymore. I got the station right away. I told the girl over the phone—*I just can't listen to Kate Smith plead any*

more. If I hadn't bought, I would have felt terrible. I would have had to shut her off."

Divided Loyalties

We have repeatedly noted that the purchase of war bonds is often imbued with symbolic significance. It is *not* a self-contained "economic" act occurring in an interpersonal and social vacuum. On the contrary, it is infected with multiple symbolisms. For some, it is at once an expression of patriotic sentiments; a testimonial to a deep-lying attachment to a parentlike figure; a quasi-magical procedure for protecting sons or brothers exposed to danger; a symbol of participation in a significant joint endeavor with an indefinitely large number of like-minded members of one's in-group; a device for allaying a cumulative sense of guilt. Furthermore, the war bond purchase takes place within another framework of interpersonal relations—relations between the bond buyer and the groups or individuals from whom the purchase is made.

People have been buying defense and war bonds for over five years. In addition to establishing mere habit patterns of purchase which have no affective significance—purchases at certain banks, theaters, post offices—many people have come to develop feelings of loyalty to particular individual or group distributors of bonds. But the act of a bond purchase, though it involves a monetary transaction, differs radically from ordinary financial transactions in its symbolic overtones. Since national bond campaigns have set forth quotas for states, cities, neighborhoods and various organizations, failure to meet these quotas is taken to indicate imperfect identification with the larger national effort. For many Americans, then, each bond purchase is surcharged with a variety of symbolic meanings. A bond pledge to an appropriate subgroup—ethnic or religious or community or occupational—testifies that the subgroup is fully integrated with the nation at large. Since individuals have multiple group affiliations, they thus become the locus of conflicting loyalties, with social pressures being exerted upon them by the several groups to which they belong. Under these conditions, each bond purchase is virtually a symbolic expression of primary loyalty to one or another group. The secondary or derivative meanings of a bond purchase thus lead to a pattern of behavior common in the sphere of morally and affectively significant conduct: means become transformed into ends. The quota system, initially intended only to further the sale of bonds, becomes the center of emotional concern. Bonds themselves become converted into a symbol of loyalty of the purchaser and of the groups with which he has significant relations.

When questioned concerning their bond-buying practices, more than a third of the poll sample indicated a concern with the quota system. Against this background of established

TABLE 5

Do you usually buy bonds to help some person
or group meet their quota?

	%
Yes	38
No	62
Total	100
No. of cases	978

loyalties, Smith's appeals introduced a conflict of obligations. In effect, she was not only asking for a bond pledge but, in many instances, for a withdrawal of allegiance from other groups and individuals. The singular emphasis of the bond campaign upon group quotas made for an environment of competing ties, in which purchasers virtually declared their primary allegiance to one or another social relationship:

"I would have bought one from her if I didn't live out of the state. *After all, we had our own quota to fill.* I thought it was just as patriotic to help fill *my own* quota as the quota of another state."

"I wouldn't want to buy bonds outside of this neighborhood. There's a quota we have. It's fair when you live in a community that you should patronize the community."

It is difficult to gauge the intensity of such conflicts of obligation. A glance at the distribution of the loyalties reported by our poll group, however, enables us to draw a few conclusions.

TABLE 6

Established Obligations for Bond Quotas

	%
Workplace	43
Specific persons (self, relatives, friends)	21
Voluntary organizations (including church)	12
Unions	8
Schools	8
Community	4
Other	4
Total per cent	100
Total cases	377

Patterned obligations to the workplace occur most frequently, for it is here that direct, unremitting social pressure can perhaps be most effectively exercised. Judging from our interviews, these commitments do not so much involve strong feelings of loyalty as a requirement to be satisfied if status is to be maintained. "The Police Department *expects* its men to buy bonds there during drives."

In contrast, established obligations to individuals often served as a genuine block to purchases from any other source. "The funny thing is that I called in for a fifty-dollar bond, and when my husband came in, he said he was selling bonds, so I said, 'I can't let you down . . . I had to split it.' " Similarly with community loyalties:

> "I did hesitate because I sort of wanted to give it to the borough. I mean, I think a person should be loyal to their borough, and why should Manhattan have the credit?"

And so, too, with loyalties to voluntary organizations:

> "I thought I'd buy an extra bond from my own organization. I felt very much that I would like to buy from Kate Smith. . . . I happen to know that all these things are recorded and credited. It's fictitious credit, but I felt I would like to have added to her credit. *But I felt I would have been traitorous to my own group.*"

From all this, we can conclude that in many instances the texture of established loyalties resisted the displacement of bond pledges to Smith. Many who were persuaded by her broadcasts failed to carry their attitude into action as a consequence of other, more enduring loyalties.[12]

---

[12] It would be a distinct contribution to our understanding of social structure were we able to determine the general grounds on which certain personal or group affiliations take precedence over others in such situations of conflicting loyalties. But our materials do not lend themselves to a solution of this problem, which, in its most general terms, has yet to be formulated. Interestingly enough, the same problem emerges in researches of political behavior in which it is found that persons ordinarily vote in accord with certain of their group affiliates. But no general formulation has been devised to account for the greater potency of particular group affiliations. See Lazarsfeld, Berelson and Gaudet, *The People's Choice*, pp. 137–149.

When men are no longer united among themselves by firm and lasting ties, it is impossible to obtain the co-operation of any great number of them unless you can persuade every man whose help you require that his private interest obliges him voluntarily to unite his exertions to the exertions of all the others. This can be habitually and conveniently effected only by means of a newspaper [dated: 1835]; nothing but a newspaper can drop the same thought into a thousand minds at the same moment. A newspaper is an adviser that does not require to be sought, but that comes of its own accord and talks to you briefly every day of the common weal, without distracting you from your private affairs.

—Alexis de Tocqueville, *Democracy in America*, II, p. 111
(Bradley ed., 1945)

Such, then, is the pattern of our American culture: A pattern of opportunity and of frustration, of strength and of careless disregard for patent weaknesses; a pattern which presents, from the vital point of view of liveability defined in terms of the satisfaction of individual rhythms and growth, a large measure of inversion of emphasis between means and end; a pattern of competing individuals struggling singlehanded in exaggeratedly big and little, and structurally defective, ant-heaps; of rootless people wandering from farm to city in quest of gain; with youth favored but frustrated, and sex roles in conflict; believing in a future which for most of them will never happen; searching for 'the way,' which recurrently turns out to be an unmarked fork in the road; and relying on the outworn dogmas of 'rational human choice' and the automaticity of 'whatsoever things are good and true' to bring them to the Promised Land. It is in the main a pattern of lack of pattern, marked by the disorder and the substitution of doing for feeling that characterizes a frontier boom town. For the individual it is a pattern of extreme complexity, contradictoriness, and insecurity.

—Robert S. Lynd, *Knowledge for What?*, p. 105

Chapter 6

THE SOCIAL AND CULTURAL CONTEXT

THE RICH and emotionally colored images of Smith, as we have seen, did not emerge full-fashioned on the day of the marathon, but for the most part long antedated it. To be sure, responses were affected by what she had to say during that day but they were also strongly influenced by previously established images of Smith and by personal ties to her. Were we to halt our inquiry at this point, without examining the sources of the cultural values which the Smith public image seemingly incorporates, it would be seriously inadequate and partially misleading. We have now to examine the social and cultural context of the sentiments of which Smith was the focus; to consider the nature of the social structure in which these sentiments found support; to investigate, in short, the ramifications of this one episode of mass persuasion into the larger reaches of the society in which it took place.

What, for example, is the social context of the enormous emphasis laid by our informants upon Smith's presumed sincerity? Why does the presence or absence of this quality loom so large among their concerns? It would appear that certain needs were satisfied by the belief in her integrity. What has given rise to these needs? Similar questions can be raised about the further components of the public images of Smith.

So, too, we have learned that Smith's large following played a considerable role in the effectiveness of her bond drive. But need the existence of this following be taken as a brute fact, or can we discover its bases in certain aspects of American culture and social structure? By searching out the functions which Smith fulfills for her adherents, we may partly account for the large measure of their devotion. Whereas in our previous discussion we were chiefly concerned with the dynamics of the persuasion episode itself, we are now looking into the social and cultural bases of the public images which entered so richly into the process of persuasion and of the mass following on which Smith could draw for support in the course of her bond drive.

The Context of Distrust

A heavy emphasis on Smith's sincerity occurs throughout our interviews.[1] It is significant that often this intense belief is expressed by informants who go on to contrast her integrity with the pretenses, deceptions and dissembling which they observe in their daily experience. On every side, they feel themselves the object of manipulation. They see themselves as the target for ingenious methods of control, through advertising which cajoles, promises, terrorizes; through propagandas that, utilizing available techniques, guide the unwitting audience into opinions which may or may not coincide with the best interests of themselves or their affiliates; through cumulatively subtle methods of salesmanship which may simulate values common to both salesman and client for private and self-interested motives. In place of a sense of *Gemeinschaft*—genuine community of values—there intrudes *pseudo-Gemeinschaft* —the feigning of personal concern with the other fellow in order to manipulate him the better. Best sellers provide popular instruction in the arts of pseudo-Gemeinschaft: "how to influence people through the pretense of friendship." Drawn

[1] See Chapter 4, pp. 82–89.
Cf. Ernst Kris, "Some Problems of War Propaganda," *The Psychoanalytic Quarterly*, 1943, 12, 381–99.

from a highly competitive, segmented urban society, our informants live in a climate of reciprocal distrust which, to say the least, is not conducive to stable human relationships. As one informant phrased it, "In my own business I can see how a lot of people in their business deals will make some kind of gesture of friendliness, sincerity and so forth, most of which is phony."

All this gives expression to some of the psychological effects of a society which, focused on capital and the market, tends to instrumentalize human relationships. In such a society, as Marx long since indicated, and as Durkheim and Simmel came to see, there are few dependable ties between each man and others. In such a society "men will tend to look at every relationship through a tradesman's eyes. They will tend more and more to picture natural objects as commodities and look at personal relationships from a mercenary point of view. In this process those much-discussed psychological phenomena, self-estrangement and dehumanization, will develop and a type of man is born for whom a tree is not a tree, but timber."[2] As codes regulating this money-centered behavior decay, there develops acute distrust of the dependability and sincerity of the other. Society is experienced as an arena for rival frauds. There is little belief in the disinterestedness of human conduct. As a devotee of Smith put it, "There are people who wouldn't lift their foot for their country. Everybody wants to make money. This city here is money-mad, dear."

The very same society that produces this sense of alienation and estrangement generates in many a craving for reassurance, an acute need to believe, a flight into faith. For her adherents, Smith has become the object of this faith. She is seen as genuine by those who seek redemption from the spurious. Her motives

[2] Karl Mannheim, *Man and Society in an Age of Reconstruction* (New York: Harcourt, Brace & Company, 1940), p. 19.

rise above avarice, ambition and pride of class. The image formed of her is the product of deep-lying needs and serves the function of temporary reassurance.[2a]

The emotional emphasis placed on Smith's "really meaning what she says" derives from the assumption that advertisers, public relations counsels, salesmen, promoters, script writers, politicians and, in extreme cases, ministers, doctors, and teachers are systematically manipulating symbols in order to gain power or prestige or income. It is the expression of a wish to be considered as a person rather than a potential client or customer. It is a reaction against the feelings of insecurity that stem from the conviction that others are dissembling and pretending to good-fellowship only to gain one's confidence and make one more susceptible to manipulation. It is, finally, the expectable response of persons living in a society which has lost many common values, which has foregone a sense of community ("Gemeinschaft") and has substituted for this community of outlook either the avowed play of atomistic personal interests within narrowly construed legal rules of the game ("Gesellschaft") or, even more disruptive to feelings of security, the mere pretense of common values in order to further private interests ("pseudo-Gemeinschaft"). And, since it is no easy task to discriminate between the pretense and the reality,

[2a] Judging from a recently observed parallel instance, we may conjecture that the concern with "sincerity" becomes widespread precisely in those situations where there is acute danger of one's being manipulated by others for their own private interests. Put too succinctly, perhaps, widespread distrust heightens sensitivity to sincerity as a social value. Thus it has been noticed that among Negroes, "the whole business of 'advancing The Race' offers wide opportunities for fraud, graft and chicanery. There are opportunities for 'selling out to the white folks,' diverting funds from 'the cause,' or making a racket out of race." It is just this social situation which lends itself to manipulation of groups by self-interested persons and that generates an exaggerated concern with sincerity: "When the people are asked to describe a 'real Race Leader' they always stress 'sincerity' as a cardinal virtue ..." St. Clair Drake and Horace R. Cayton, *Black Metropolis: A Study of Negro Life in a Northern City* (New York: Harcourt, Brace and Company, 1945), pp. 392–93.

there is an avid search for cues which testify to the one or the other. Hence, the enormous importance of Smith's "propaganda of the deed" as distinct from her "propaganda of the word." She not only talks, she acts. She not only praises benevolence and generosity, she apparently exemplifies them. It is these behavioral cues that are seized upon as evidence of her full-fashioned sincerity. "If everyone would follow her with their hearts, everything would be all right," a Smith disciple assures us. The phrasing is suggestive: if only Smith, the steadfast symbol of integrity, were taken as the prototype of behavior, insecurities could be allayed. And the reassurance function of the Smith image in an atmosphere of pervasive distrust is further expressed by a follower who exclaims: "I trust her. If *she* were a fake, I'd feel terrible."

The Smith following, then, is no mere aggregate of persons who are entertained by a popular singer. For many, she has become the symbol of a moral leader who "demonstrates" by her own behavior that there need be no discrepancy between appearance and reality in the sphere of human relationships. That an entertainer should have captured the moral loyalties of so large a following is itself an incisive commentary on prevailing social and political orientations.[3] But the gratifications

[3] Compare a recent study which found a shift, during the last generation, in the nature of the "heroes" of biographies in popular magazines. Whereas the earlier subjects of biographies were "idols of production"—stemming from industry, business and scientific research—the latter-day heroes are "idols of consumption"—being drawn almost wholly from the realm of entertainment and sport. "While we found that around 1900 and even around 1920 the vocational distribution of magazine heroes was a rather accurate reflection of the nation's living trends, we observe that today the hero-selection corresponds to needs quite different from those of genuine information. They seem to lead to a dream world of the masses who no longer are capable or willing to conceive of biographies primarily as a means of orientation and education. *They receive information not about the agents and methods of social production but about the agents and methods of social and individual consumption.* During the leisure in which they read, they read almost exclusively about people who are directly, or indirectly, providing for the reader's leisure time. The vocational set-up of the dramatis personae is or-

which Smith provides for her adherents are not confined to this one type of reassurance. We have seen that Smith presents a kaleidoscopic set of images to her audience: she is at once patriot and philanthropist, mother, spiritual guide and mentor. And, not to be forgotten, she is both a successful careerist and a homebody. Though these images differ in detail, and indeed at times seem to be at odds with one another, they provide a diversity of gratifications for those who are themselves not overly secure in a success-oriented culture.

Lilith Rejected

It has been suggested that the American culture defines three prevailing models for the feminine sex role: the domesticity pattern, the career pattern, and the glamour pattern.[4] The co-existence of these patterns, which call for somewhat incompatible interests and behavior, often leads to serious strains upon those women who do not cleave fully to one or another of them. For many of her adherents, Smith serves to mitigate this strain and conflict by reinforcing one of these patterns at the expense of the others. By examining the processes through which she fulfills this psychological function, we may be able to account further for her mass following.

More than half of our informants spontaneously alluded to Smith's physical appearance: she is described as a large, stout woman who neither possesses nor makes any apparent effort to achieve sexual allure. In this limited erotic sense, she is viewed almost as sexless. She is neither beautiful (indeed, comfortingly fat) nor disturbingly "cultured" (with the attendant hostilities

ganized as if the social production process were either completely exterminated or tacitly understood, and needed no further interpretation." Leo Lowenthal, "Biographies in Popular Magazines," in *Radio Research, 1942-1943* (ed. by P. F. Lazarsfeld and Frank Stanton) (New York: Duell, Sloan & Pearce, 1944), pp. 516-518.

[4] Talcott Parsons, "Age and Sex in the Social Structure of the United States," *American Sociological Review*, 7 (1942), 604-616.

which upper-class-typed voices often evoke). In affectionate summary, "she's just fat, plain Kate Smith."

The overtones of solace and relief accompanying these descriptions of Smith suggest the gratifications that stem from her mere appearance. In a culture which has capitalized the glamour pattern,[5] Smith fans who do not measure up to the cultural expectations of feminine attractiveness find in her a gratifying basis for comparison. In contrast to the Hollywood starlet whose stylized, glamourized "beauty" elicits invidious self-comparisons, Smith is no target for hostility. "Joan Bennett —she's just a dressed-up doll. All she can do is model clothes. Have you noticed that? But I just like Kate Smith—I think she's a marvelous woman." Her adherents gratefully point to her self-evident repudiation of standards of glamour and sexual allure and her reinforcement of the domesticity pattern. A thirty-year-old mother whose obesity became pronounced after the birth of her second child, gives clear expression to the psychological functions served by Smith: "*Take some of these actresses, do they care about anything but themselves? Many of these actresses are beautiful, lovely figures, but Kate Smith hasn't any of this. To her, beauty isn't everything. She's just herself.*" And further: "*I look on this as a mother: I don't want beauty. Perhaps at sixteen I wanted it, or at nineteen, but now I don't want it any more.* [In agitated tones] *I'm thinking of my children, I'm not thinking of glamour* [said with withering contempt]."

Smith is taken as a living testimonial that the cultural accent on feminine attractiveness may be safely abandoned. In tones

[5] Parsons refers to the "glamour pattern, with the emphasis on a specifically feminine form of attractiveness which on occasion involves directly sexual patterns of appeal." He suggests further "that in a situation which strongly inhibits competition between the sexes on the same plane the feminine glamour pattern has appeared as an offset to masculine occupational status and to its attendant symbols of prestige." *Ibid.*, pp. 610–611.

almost of startled relief, informants draw the inescapable moral that sexual allure is no essential basis for popularity: "She certainly does appeal to the youth of today and that's remarkable for a woman who's not the actress type. *Considering she's so stout and all, her figure wouldn't appeal to a young person* . . . [musingly] . . . *l mean men, you know* . . . *and yet,* she's a great favorite with the Army and Navy when she goes around the camps and sings for them."

And as "plain Kate Smith" her array of the more "homespun" moral values coupled with her lack of concern with glamour enable her fans to reappraise themselves more favorably than when drawing comparisons between themselves and the more glamourous stars. Furthermore, Smith subscribes to the cultural ideal of the woman as essentially a key unit in the family as wife and mother, and has little to say about women who follow careers. She thus provides emotional support for those who are confined to the occasionally cramping role of housewife and mother, for those who are shut off from occupational achievement. In effect, Smith assures them that their present role offers more than the gains which they may attribute to the successful career woman.

Nor is there any paradox in Smith, herself a career woman, performing this function. For, tacitly, it is inferred that she would probably like nothing better than the role of wife and mother. She is the old maid—"after all, she's not a young girl"— the involuntary spinster, thwarted in the "natural" desire of every woman to have a husband and children. For this lonely state, her success and fame are but poor compensation. It is not that she has willingly eschewed marital and maternal joys as have many women in the world of affairs—she is a career woman in spite of her wishes. Hence she is more to be pitied than envied. "*If only she could be a mommy*—she should have six kids."

Smith as Mother Figure

Of all the Smith images, this would at first blush seem the most improbable. For it is well known to her audience that she is not married. Yet sixteen of the hundred informants spontaneously comment on the motherliness of the spinster Smith. Her marital status is seldom called into question in connection with her mother virtues—her symbolic maternalism transcends such an irrelevant point.

The statements of those who regard Smith as a mother symbol suggest the sources of this image. One factor, of course, is her appearance. "She has a real motherly look." "To me, she is a plump little mother." But "plumpness" per se is not the central component of the mother symbol. (Sophie Tucker, who qualifies abundantly in this respect, is probably never imagined in this way—she is, rather, a "red-hot momma.") Other attributes are clustered in this image. A devout Catholic mother who sees Smith in this role observes: "She's so *clean* . . . her character has always been so clean and lovely. There's never been a blemish since she started in show business, she's a credit to show business and radio." Smith escapes the dubiously moral associations of the glamour pattern: "the temperamental ones, the glamour girls couldn't do what she did."

The configuration of virtue and lack of glamour approximates the mother image standardized in our culture. For such a conception is perhaps most vitally related to the *asexual* aspect which these qualities suggest. It has long been emphasized in psychoanalytic circles that a common fantasy in childhood is the belief that one's parents do not have sexual intercourse. It is not surprising, therefore, that to see Smith as a mother is to stress the asexual aspects of her public personality. "*You never hear of anything wrong with her*. I think she's the old-fashioned kind of girl like they used to have in the 1890's . . ."

"This may be putting it to extremes. . . . She's almost like a saintly person. . . . Innocence, you would call it."

Closely linked with Smith as mother surrogate is her role as guide and mentor. A Mother must know best. The mother image apparently derives from idealized versions of the early parental figures. "Years ago, my mother used to speak and say the same words Miss Smith does." In extreme instances, she is endowed with omniscience and understanding. "You know what she says is true. Next to God she comes when she tells it to you." As mentor, she assumes the authoritative role of the Stern Mother. "She was strong talking, serious talking. She talk how the mother talk to the children." Or, she becomes an agent of socialization, explaining the moral imperatives. "She's one of those motherly types protecting her children. *We're her children, all her children. She's like a mother who just wants you to understand.*" And, on occasion, she assumes the role of the Tender Mother. "She isn't a mother, but, by gosh, she talks like a mother; she sounds as if she loves them all." Again, her reputation for benevolence reinforces the mother image. "She takes interest in everybody—poor families here and there. . . . A good mother who has twelve children and keeps them all under her wings, that's how I picture her."

The projective character of the mother image is indicated by a variety of data. More than one in five mothers and only one of 16 other women spontaneously referred to this image in the interviews. The intimations suggested by these figures are supported by data from the poll of 978 persons: only 5 per cent of other female informants in contrast to 10 per cent of mothers with sons in service selected the phrase, "a motherly kind of person," as most descriptive of Smith.

It appears further that the mother image is more frequent among the lower than the higher income strata. Nor is this a result of differences in educational level, as the following chart indicates. On each educational level, there are significantly more instances of the mother-image among the lower income group.

CHART IV

Proportions of Smith Mother Images Among Informants on Different Educational and Income Levels

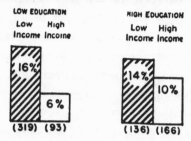

This suggests a further possible function of this image. One may hazard the hypothesis that low income is more likely to produce a sense of dependence and need for the kind of sympathetic solicitude represented by the maternal figure.

The role of the press agent and organized publicity in fostering the maternal image of Smith cannot be ignored. Symbolism transcends the facts of the case. Her spinsterhood does not preclude an honorary life membership in the Blue Star Mothers of America. In the modern Pantheon, Kate Smith is the goddess of the household. The advertisements show her, plump and rosy-cheeked in a neat white apron, at work in the kitchen. And on June 17, 1944, the press carried an account that the "National Father's Day Committee"—their membership and authorization not being indicated in the article—had awarded the "coveted" Eisenhower medal to Kate Smith because she had labored successfully "to cement fine relationships" between fathers and their children. This again capitalizes on Smith's domesticity role and lack of glamour. Whatever else the pin-up girls may contribute to the life of father, they could hardly be given an award for strengthening his ties to his children.

Class Structure and Success

When we first talked with our informants, we had little reason to suppose that considerations of social class would enter into the process of being persuaded to buy a war bond. Rather, since war bonds presumably serve as a symbol of national unity, their purchase would be expected to occur within a context of common feelings transcending class lines. It is of some interest, then, that forty-one of our hundred informants *spontaneously* alluded to their own or Smith's class position in discussing their response to her bond drive. In exploring the sources of this tendency to import class orientations into this situation, we may come to see more closely the sense in which Smith's faithful following is an outgrowth of needs induced by American society.

It has often been stated that Americans will not publicly recognize that our society is stratified into several social classes. Or, if recognition is reluctantly given, the edge of class differences is blunted by most people ascribing middle-class position to themselves. This public exorcism of social classes could readily prevail, and not only on ceremonial occasions, so long as an expanding economy provided ample scope for rapid social mobility. If men did not stay long enough in any one class to be permanently tagged, obviously, then, classes were arbitrarily fixed points in a continuous movement up the social hierarchy. No matter if social ascent were not as widespread as popular belief would have it—most could point to the case of "a man who made good." The conviction became rooted that yesterday's office boy was tomorrow's boss and this became stylized into the belief that, in this country at least, social classes did not exist.

But, irrespective of the belief in social ascent, it appears that the rate of vertical mobility has in fact been declining.[6] As opportunities have become more limited, as mass unemployment convinced many that upward, ever upward might be better regarded as a dream than a prospect, as more and more people were compelled to recognize that they would, in all probability, remain in the socioeconomic stratum in which they were born, if indeed they could maintain this status at all, there developed an increasing concern with and consciousness of class position. When ambitions continue to be fed both by precept and by occasional example, the individual finds himself chafing under the frustrations which he experiences in seeking to thrust himself up the social ladder. School and home and advertising continue to stimulate the objective of "getting ahead." Those who fail to make the next higher grade or the one beyond that come to look for the explanation in their own inadequacy.[7] The partial closure of the class system is thus experienced as personal distress and occasional exceptions only aggravate the feeling of having somehow failed to achieve the expected.

It is within such a social context, apparently, that Smith takes on special significance for her following. Her devoted fans take one metaphor literally: they have hitched their wagon to a

[6] In *Middletown in Transition*, Robert S. and Helen M. Lynd show that in one American community: (1) the ladder has lost lower rungs with the disappearance of apprenticeship; (2) the step up to the foreman level is more difficult; (3) the higher personnel are not recruited from the laborers, but come in over another route; (4) the enterprising workman finds it increasingly difficult to get the capital required to launch a new enterprise on an appropriate scale; (5) local plants are being absorbed in large national corporations; (6) intermarriage among the financial elite links the big fortunes by social ties which are seldom "crashed" from below. They refer to the long-term trend as contracting "working-class hopes to the permanent boundaries of nineteen-dollar suits, $2.50 shoes, and a second-hand Chevie." See p. 71 f.

[7] E. W. Bakke, *The Unemployed Worker* (Yale University Press, 1940). For a parallel account of the class context of manipulative behavior, see Arnold W. Green, "Duplicity," *Psychiatry*, 6 (1943), 411–24.

star. She is viewed as a prototype of the American saga: an individual who has climbed from the lower reaches of the economic ladder virtually to the topmost rung. Without formal training, she has so utilized her talents as to prove her worth. All this seemingly testifies to the fact that careers are still open to talents, whatever one's doubts on this score may have been. For her "identification public,"[8] Smith's example provides a renewed sense of what one might well have become. *"I hear she sings without training and she's gone ahead and made a success. I admire her for it. I could've been like Kate, if I was given the opportunity. I have a very strong, sweet voice."*

Not only does Smith's career testify to rapid mobility in what might otherwise be experienced as a world of contracting opportunity, but informants manifest a vicarious pride in her achievements. This reflected glory is evident in the frequent comments of the "I knew her when" variety. Smith's every step upward is experienced as virtually an achievement of the informant herself. For those who identify themselves with Smith, her success becomes their success. "You know, my brother-in-law remembers her when she lived on Jerome Avenue. That time, she must've weighed 140 pounds. She came into his store to buy some material. She was starting her career then. I take an interest in her as if she was my sister; I know when she got her short haircut." Reflected glory becomes a source, however indirect and tenuous it may seem to the observer, of personal gratification. This is the soil in which "fan

[8] "One of the most crowd-minded types of publics might be called the *identification public*. This type of public is characterized by its idolatry of some person or group. . . . The common factor in all such identification publics is the release of frustrated attitudes and feelings of inferiority, undoubtedly a function of the culture at that time. The idol generally epitomizes the frustrated aims and ambitions of the individual." Daniel Katz and R. L. Schanck, *Social Psychology* (New York: John Wiley & Sons, 1938), pp. 605–606.

clubs" proliferate, in which those who have not validated their own claims to achievement may vicariously share in the success pattern of "their" rising star.

And these devoted followers seize upon every testimonial to their vicariously experienced success. The celebrated Smith, we are told, is free to move among the great. Even the most lofty in station acknowledge her attainments. "You know, I heard from what you really call reliable sources, that *President Roosevelt doesn't miss her programs on Friday*. During the day, he hasn't enough time to listen to her. *She was a guest there, you know, when Queen what'sa name was there*."

Equality and Self-respect

The saving grace for Smith is that, despite her success, she is "unspoiled." She has not forgotten her humble origins, she apparently retains an identification with the common man. "*She's not high-hat, nor stuck-up. She mingles with everyone.* She takes interest in poor people and I like a person like that." "Nothin' stuck-up about her—she's sociable with everyone."

A devoted follower, who feels herself rebuffed by her successful sister—"very high-class people"—comments with fervor on Smith's apparent accessibility to all, whatever their status. "She speaks with her heart and soul. *She seems to be friendly, interested in people's troubles.* She tells stories about poor people, sick people. . . . *She's really friends for everybody.*" The personal context of these remarks can be more fully appreciated when we learn that this person feels herself neglected by her wealthy sister, while faced with the crises of her husband's death and her daughter's illness. It is not difficult to understand how this informant, abandoned by her "successful" sister, finds satisfaction in the presumed friendliness, sympathy and accessibility of the even more successful Smith. Smith apparently challenges the pattern of the socially mobile person who, with each move upward, dissociates herself from the ties and relationships which might hamper her further ascent. Though she is free to associate with "big people," she adheres to her folksy speech and provincial ways. By identifying herself with the plain folk in her audience, she counters their possible feelings of inferiority. She reaffirms her primary attachment to her origins. Or, in the more expressive words of an admirer, "She's not a high-toned little mug."

Symbolizing her role as "just one of us" is her chummy, neighborly greeting: "Hello, folks" or "Hello, everybody." She reminds us that she has no pretensions to grandiosity or highfalutin' ways. As she put it in her bond drive:

> "I haven't any stories or fancy phrases to fling at you . . . no sound effects to capture your attention. *I'm a plain simple woman.*"

And Smith's adherents are quick to seize upon this absence of pretension: "You know, sometimes you meet another person and *they say the same things as your own family does,* and they're sincere about it. You feel that you'd like to go up and grab her and tell her how much you like her. That's what I'd like to do to her."

It is this rejection of pretensions that especially endears Smith to many who resent the claims of others to superior status. "She takes an interest in everybody. *No other actor or actress would do that, I assure you.*" Since she expresses a feeling of being on the same plane with them, they can identify themselves wholeheartedly with her success. They do not need to circulate about Smith the bitter gossip unwittingly calculated to deflate the pretentious and cut them down to the speaker's size. Smith has forestalled this kind of reaction by conforming to what the American ethos demands—the successful person who is still "one of us," for whom a phenomenal increase in income does not mean a new way of life: "She's unassuming, with a wonderful personality. She never was high-hat. Money never made a great impression on her. *She never changed when she was getting fifty dollars a week and when she was getting $7,000 a week.*"

Andrew Jackson and Abraham Lincoln both serve as political prototypes of this American tradition. And indeed, her fans bring Smith into this context, seeing no incongruity in assimilating an entertainer into the company of political leaders. Social policy and dramatic symbolism are viewed as indistinguishable.

> "*I think the President is a great mind, and he and Kate are on the same level. He looks to the underdog and so does she.* I hated Herbert Hoover, who always wanted to balance the budget when people are starving."

> "She's next to the President—taking interest in everybody."

Incidentally, Smith's insistence upon her concern with ordinary folk helps considerably to sustain the impression of "sincerity." The several facets of the Smith public personality are joined into a consistent public image. As Richards has observed in this general connection: "Simplicity, we may think, has something to do with sincerity, for there is a sense in which 'genuine' is opposed to 'sophisticated.' The sincere feeling, it may be suggested, is one which has been left in its natural state, not worked over and complicated by reflection. Thus strong spontaneous feelings would be more likely to be sincere than feelings that have run the gauntlet of self-criticism. . . . Admiration for the 'spontaneous' and 'natural' tends to select favourable examples and turns a very blind eye to the less attractive phenomena. Moreover, many emotions which look simple and natural are nothing of the kind, they result from cultivated self-control, so consummate as to seem instantaneous."[9]

When adherents praise Smith's "understanding," they often seem to mean that she speaks from within the normal world view of their own perspectives. They trust her because she belongs to their own stratum. Her alleged sincerity has a social basis: it is a product of her belonging to the in-group. She is kinfolk.

By the same token, many listeners drawn from other social strata distrust Smith. Differently located in the class structure, they exhibit different attitudes toward her. She is not one of them. A well-to-do college graduate expresses this sense of social distance: "She appeals to the masses; she has no message for *me*." Her language is not their language and for them her sentimentality rings false and her "folksy" manner is rejected as class-typed and "vulgar." "Strictly *entre-nous*, I think she's terribly low-class." "I can't stand that low-class vulgarity."

The fact that Smith, known by many to have a fabulous income, can reject "pretensions" does far more to validate the status of ordinary people than would similar assertions by those who have no claims to higher status. Smith, presumably given the option of moving in upper-class circles, ostensibly proves through her public behavior that those who do not have this option need not regard themselves as "failures." Smith, in the eyes of her devoted listeners, is the polar opposite of the *nouveaux riches* who seek to climb out of their "own" social class, repudiating the values of the stratum they leave behind. "She seems like she's herself—*not as if she's trying to be somebody else*. Just a human being. *She's just our everyday people.*"

How is this "plain folks" atmosphere achieved? For one thing, her vocabulary is severely limited to the few thousand

[9] I. A. Richards, *Practical Criticism* (London: Kegan Paul, Trench, Trubner & Co., 1929), p. 282.

words most commonly used. A housewife, who herself occasionally experiments with less familiar terms, comments that "she doesn't delve into the deep art of the mystery of words or speech. She talks plain, common-sense English that anybody can understand."

Again, the subject matter of her talks contributes to this atmosphere. We have previously noted the halo that develops from Smith's frequent use of the word "American" and her identification with the song "God Bless America," and that these practices are in part responsible for her reputation as a patriot. So, too, her repeated anecdotes of plain, run-of-the-mill people reflect back upon her, the narrator, until she also becomes a plain, everyday person for her audience. In her war bond drive, she continued her practice of being a spokesman for the "little man":

> "Here's one little incident I heard about—*the story of a poor man that may well put many a richer, more successful man to shame.*"

> "I've got a story to tell you . . . another story about another American. This one's an elevator operator in a big office building, and I think he's a very special American . . ."

And the informant quoted earlier in this chapter who observed that "she tells stories about poor people . . . she's really friends for everybody," nicely summarizes the mechanism of the halo. Smith's tales of "poor, sick people" are taken as *proof* of her own status as an "ordinary" person.

Responses to Smith's nominal repudiation of the rights and perquisites of her achieved station in life must be interpreted within the American social and cultural context. For ours is a culture in which the yardstick of "success" is used to measure oneself as well as others.[10] Subjected to a ceaseless barrage of

---

[10] Lasswell and Mead have some perceptive observations in this connection. Harold D. Lasswell, *Personality, Culture and Education* (mimeographed, 1939), p. 31; Margaret Mead, *And Keep Your Powder Dry* (New York: William Morrow & Co., 1942), Chapter VII.

ratings by parents and teachers, by employers and associates, Americans are exposed to considerable stress and strain. In this atmosphere, status anxiety becomes normal. Radio quizzes and self-evaluation devices in mass magazines capitalize on this concern with measuring one's own comparative standings; intelligence tests and aptitude tests and tests of every description press insistently for self-appraisals. "How do I measure up?" becomes a culturally standardized phrase. As a consequence, this is a culture which continuously batters the ego of the "unsuccessful."

But among her adherents, Smith reduces the impact of such devastating self-appraisals. For here is Smith who, by virtue of what are taken as signal achievements, could be condescending and aloof, yet is not. Her expressed attitudes appear to challenge the bases for such invidious self-judgments. She validates the humble station by insisting that she seeks nothing else for herself. She becomes an active source of gratification for those who, lacking the outward and visible marks of success, run the risk of suffering the contempt of others and, derivatively, of themselves.

An Ideological Balm

All this suggests further functions which Smith fulfills for her followers. She is the custodian of the ever-old values that can replace the goal of success. She provides a substitute frame for self-judgment. "Not wealth," she says in effect, "not power or prominence, but old-fashioned virtue: this alone matters." She doesn't talk to the home folks of America about social prominence, business success, or Hollywood romance. Instead, she affirms and reaffirms the homely virtues. By this measuring rod many who claim worldly success will fall short and the economically disadvantaged can still win stars for their crowns. Self-esteem need not be made contingent upon economic success. Not all can be wealthy but all *can* be kind and forebearing. However deprived one may be, there are always the more fully dispossessed, and charity for these—a doll for the orphan, a sandwich for the beggar—validates one's position in the hierarchy of virtue. Self-feelings of inadequacy can be mitigated by looking with compassion upon those who are even closer to being "down and out." Lower-class adherents of Smith echo these sentiments: *"At times she takes the gloom out of life. There are hundreds of people worse off than we are, so we never need to feel that life is gloomy."* "People are sick and they make you feel how much better off you are. Others are down and you're not so bad off." An elderly widow who identifies herself as "poor class" reports: "I'm great for sharing with poor people; they can't help themselves. *Kate Smith is great for charity; I done a lot of charity in my life.* If you got twenty-five cents, you can share it. I see old men begging in the street. I take 'em into a restaurant. Kate Smith's got the same feeling about poor people like I do."

In order to obtain further understanding of the psychological functions served by this substitution of "moral" standards for "success" standards as a basis for self-judgment, interview questions of a "projective" type were designed to lead informants to elaborate their attitudes and feelings about their own economic position. Do the responses of Smith adherents suggest the gratifications which they may derive from her "philosophy of life?" Does she provide psychological balm for those who are economically or socially disadvantaged? The following question provided a springboard for comments which indicated the informant's attitudes toward monetary goals, his own aspirations, readiness to adopt other than monetary criteria for self-appraisals, and so on.

What do you think about this statement: "In the long run, rich people are not any happier than poor people"?

Of the sixty persons interviewed on this point, more than three-quarters agreed with the statement on one basis or another. And though the paucity of cases provides no secure basis for statistical analysis, there is a discernible tendency for Smith fans more often to assent to the view that the rich are not any happier than the poor. Of the forty informants who listen regularly to her noonday programs, thirty-four express agreement with the statement, in comparison with thirteen of the twenty who hear her program occasionally or not at all. The same differences in proportion hold for those who are "devoted" to Smith and for those who are either indifferent or hostile.

More illuminating than these slight figures are the characteristic expressions of opinion stemming from the Smith fans. Of course, we cannot say definitely that Smith creates these sentiments which heighten the self-esteem of those who are not well to do. It may well be that her programs attract those who would, in any case, hold to such beliefs. In view of the content of her programs, however, it is likely that she reinforces these sentiments for some and possibly instills them in others. In fact, the comments of her disciples sound very much like her own homilies: "Home life, and how your children come out, and how you get along with your husband—that's more important than money." "The only thing that satisfies is a clear conscience, a happy home and family."

Not only does Smith have much the same value definitions, but she makes it easier for the disadvantaged to decry the value of wealth. To repudiate what one does not have can too easily be interpreted as sour grapes. But for a Kate Smith, so liberally blessed with worldly goods, to depreciate wealth as a sham and meretricious value gives firm support to such repudiations. Lower income listeners to Smith's admonitions that nonpecuniary values are the true values can the more readily become reconciled to their own situation. They may come to phrase enforced austerity of life as a definite asset.

The nature of such sentiments is reflected in the comments of informants who explain why the rich are not happier than the poor. There is a strong moral overtone in discussing "the rich." In contrast to the poor, they fail to experience the basic satisfactions of stable family life.

> "*I figure money isn't everything in life, after all. They [the rich] don't have the comfort in their home and family that poorer people do,* especially in that their children are handed over to other people."

> "The average wealthy woman *doesn't have any close contact with her children, if she has any, or with her husband.* She just doesn't know what real happiness is."

The rich not only lack positive satisfaction of home and children. They exhibit a tendency toward immorality, reflected in divorce and separations, which grow out of the "fast life" which they lead.

> "*People with a great deal of money start seeking pleasure outside.* You go out and leave yourself open to more trouble, instead of confining yourself to home life. That accounts for a lot of these divorces and separations."

> "*The rich look for trouble and they find it*—keeping up with the Joneses, and divorces."

> "*With the rich people, there are more divorces. And 17-year-olds marrying 60-year-olds for wealth.* I don't call that a happy life. I think most people are happier than the rich."

Nor does the contrast in morality end there. The immorality of the rich involves them in a series of disasters, culminating at times in murder. Respondents seized upon the then recent murder of an heiress—the Lonergan case—to document their view that wealth brings tragedy in its wake:

> "*I think the poor people live a much happier and better life.* With all their wealth, I don't think they amount to anything. Did you read it in the papers yesterday? The 22-year-old heiress that was murdered. She was no good, I guess."

> "*How those people live!* Take the Lonergan murder. That was a terrible thing!"

In a different phrasing, wealth is seen as the prelude to other tragedies, without the keynote of immorality. The rich are viewed as peculiarly subject to kidnappings, ill-health, suicide. This is further ground for repudiating riches as a significant goal, even in a "pecuniary society." Other objectives can be substituted, since society is believed to exact too heavy a price from those on whom it bestows its largess. Part of the heavy price of possessions is found in the fears that follow hard upon wealth. Violence awaits those that have.

> "True, they're not happier. *They got more money, and they're afraid.* They're afraid someone will kill them for their money."

> "That's true. *They got more worries.* Nobody's gonna kidnap poor people like us."

Studies of the maldistribution of medical care notwithstanding, some Smith adherents are convinced that wealth is associated with ill-health. And since money "can't buy health," this sometimes becomes the ground for believing that happiness awaits the poor rather than the rich: "It's true. *They're more sick than the poor, too.*" And as most conclusive evidence that wealth and happiness are incompatible is the propensity of the rich for suicide. Ennui invites self-destruction:

> "*I think they're less happy.* They have nothing to occupy their minds. They may go to the theatre, *but when you figure how many of them jump out of windows and commit suicide.* They don't know how to spend their time."

Furthermore, many Smith fans view the daily routine of the rich as deprived of the gratifications that come from over-coming obstacles. The sheer struggle for existence is assumed to provide a zest which is its own reward. The cultural stereo-type of the "poor rich" is called into play; the bored rich are more to be pitied than envied:

"Well, they aren't. I think they are more unhappy than hap-py. *When you have everything, there's no respect for it.* They think whenever they want something, they can get it. When you've worked hard and know there's money coming in that you will be able to do the things you've wanted, it's different. I think the poor people are happier than the rich— looking forward to doing things in the future and all. I asked my husband for a bond on our wedding anniversary. I was tickled pink when he gave it to me. A rich person wouldn't ask for that and enjoy it."

"I think really the rich people are not happy. They get so many things done for them. *They don't get the zest out of life that a poor man does. You get a kick out of what you do yourself.*"

Nor is this easy satisfaction of desires the only reason why the rich are believed to have few gratifying experiences. In the fashion of Faust, their desires always outrun what they have. They are imbued with insatiable wants and aspirations and, consequently, true gratification always eludes them:

"*The rich never have enough.* They always want more."

"I don't think rich people are any happier than poor people, because *they're always reaching for more than they got.*"

This source of unhappiness is contrasted with the situation of the poor who, it is believed, strike a reasonable balance between wants and achievement. By curbing their wants and expectations, by drawing in their aspirations, the poor achieve a larger measure of happiness:

> "*They're contented with what they have.*"

> "Oh, I think it's very true. The poor people—they're not used to having so much. *They appreciate what they got.* The rich people—they're spoiled."

By the criterion of happiness, then, poverty is nothing to be deplored. Wealth is construed as the fountainhead of unhappy homes, divorce, and immorality. The rich have their own array of woes: ill-health, kidnapping, and murder. They can know little of happiness, since neither the ease of acquisition nor insatiable wants permit of gratification. Thus poverty emerges almost as a positive value. To him that hath not, happiness is given.

An Economic Credo

The comments of Smith adherents on the view that wealth does not lead to happiness at times implied an aggressive attitude toward the "the rich": they are believed to lack moral responsibility. "Look at the way they run around; how they figure in murders and suicides; how they neglect their children and go in for divorce." But, characteristically, this aggression is directed toward wealthy *people* and not toward the *institutional structure* that permits of such seeming unhappiness and moral disintegration. Rich persons are vulnerable, the institutions remain sacrosanct.[11]

Though the interpretation must remain conjectural, there

---

[11] Studies of radio "soap operas" have found the same tendency to deal with problems as a consequence of individual vices and virtues, rather than of social forces and institutions. See Rudolf Arnheim, "The World of the Daytime Serial," in *Radio Research 1942–1943* (ed. by P. F. Lazarsfeld and Frank Stanton) (New York: Duell, Sloan and Pearce, 1944), pp. 34–85; Herta Herzog, "On Borrowed Experience," *Studies in Philosophy and Social Science*, 1941, Vol. IX, No. 1.

are some indications that Smith may reinforce such perspectives among her followers. Running through the Smith noonday broadcasts has been the implication that, despite all superficial changes and challenges, our basic institutions remain sacred and stable. No breath of economic skepticism or radicalism ever appears in her talks. In order to investigate the extent to which these perspectives are reflected among her devoted listeners, they were asked to comment on another projective statement: "Do you feel that this country would be better off or worse off if the wealth were spread more evenly among the people?" Again, our interest is focused, not on their judgment of the economic practicability of such redistribution, but on the sentiments activated by the question.

From the responses, it is evident that this statement touches off a series of profoundly conservative sentiments regarding economic institutions. And though the number of cases is too few to permit of any definite conclusion, it is suggestive that 29 of 39 devoted listeners to the Smith noonday broadcast as compared with 13 of 23 nonlisteners express these sentiments. Objections are not phrased in terms of economic or technical difficulties which might attend such redistribution. Rather, they are couched in terms of an abiding faith in the "conservative credo."

For some, the proposal to "spread the wealth more evenly" is at once dismissed as running counter to the sentiments clustered about the institution of private property. Repeatedly, informants with modest incomes and possessions express the unelaborated sentiment: "*If you make money, you're entitled to it.* To have to give it to someone else, isn't right." "I figure whatever a person is eligible to make belongs to him."

The belief that only economic necessity goads people to work finds frequent expression. If security is at hand, people will promptly cease and desist from labor.

"There's lazy people and people who are willing to work *so why should the lazy people benefit from those who work?*"

"No, no. When we work we have it. If we spread it evenly, *naturally there would be 90 per cent who wouldn't work.* I believe in working for everything I get."

The wife of a shoe salesman documents the problems which arise when the firm hard pressure of need is no longer felt by workers:

"No, honey, it would never do. *Because it's even hard now. Everybody is making so much money, you can't get nobody to do your work. They're so independent.* You can't get a man to clean your windows even. My friend can't get anybody to work in the store."

This merges into the view that present differences in wealth are eminently reasonable and proper, since they are the normal outcome of differences in ability and effort. There is an unquestioned conviction that our society is so constituted that people get their just deserts. That these sentiments should be expressed by informants who are convinced of their own upper-class position is not surprising. The Englishwoman who reports her acquaintance with Sir Gerald and Lady C———, for example, might be expected to believe that those less well off than she get what they deserve:

"Darling, that you'll never change. You will always have some people who will have more money than others. These working people, *they wouldn't want money.* They wouldn't know how to act if they did have it; they have no education."

But the extent to which these sentiments are echoed by those who regard themselves as "working class" or "poor class" is even more revealing. Consider, for example, an elderly housewife, with a small income and of limited grade school education, who reaffirms the legitimacy of present arrangements:

"People with good heads deserve more. If my head isn't as good as another one, why should I get the same as you? I didn't try hard enough for it. . . . *How do people get rich? They're smarter than we are."*

A small shopkeeper, viewing herself as poised between "the rich" and "the poor," points to the essential incapacity of the poor as the chief reason for their plight:

> *"I imagine poor people are poor because most of them are poor managers.* People like us, we're more in the middle class. We don't see too much hardship. I'm very sympathetic to sick people, but *really poor people—it's always their own fault."*

The wife of a dockworker expresses her preference for present arrangements:

> "I want to tell you something. I enjoy working and I think this is the best way. That there should be wealthy people and middle class and poor. . . . *There got to be millionaires; there got to be people who have less and less. So I say, be satisfied as you are."*

And a housewife of modest means sums up this attitude in terms of its probable inherent justice:

> "I personally think it's nice the way it is. There could be some changes, but the world can't be perfect. *The people that should have it, probably have it and those that shouldn't, don't."*

The wife of a bank teller, who had herself worked as a secretary in an automobile sales company, bluntly recapitulates her attitudes:

> "I'm a capitalist at heart. I believe that labor was the underdog for years and I think we've done a lot of marvelous things for them, but I think it's swinging too far for them.

I maintain that if the man behind the machine had the brains, he'd be behind the desk. Nine out of ten of the men in labor haven't the mentality to cope with the power given them. . . . *I think everybody has a chance here. If he has initiative, he'll get ahead.* I think it [spreading wealth more evenly] would take away the initiative. There would be no incentive."

Echoing the same sentiments is the wife of another bank teller —the mother of eight children who speaks anxiously of the debts that accumulate despite her every effort. Having remarked that Smith has "overcome a lot" to succeed, she goes on to say:

"A king would rise above his surroundings, no matter what. I think as the Lord says, *we'll always have the poor and ignorant.* You'll always have a certain percentage that will be dependent. Our country is free. *Everybody has a chance.*"

And since ability and initiative inevitably find their due reward, it becomes evident that any redistribution of wealth would be only temporary, leading irresistibly to the *status quo ante.*

"If you divided it, it'd only be a little while before those who had a lot would have it again. You have to place a premium on enterprise."

Listeners refer for confirmation to Smith's human interest stories which document the ease with which people can move onward and upward. A housekeeper substantiates her views by calling to mind Smith's account of "a man who came to this country a nobody and now he is wealthy and has a business."

For her fans, Smith takes on the role of lay priestess. Her secular sermons define good and evil. "Her stories give you something to think about—it's like a sermon," says a devoted listener who feels that Smith is "really a spiritual uplift." Serving as a mentor who clarifies the problems which press in upon her followers, Smith domesticates the larger society. She screens out institutional defects and inadequacies of social organization to congeal the real world into a mass of virtuous and immoral *actions*, of good and bad *people*. Explaining her confidence in Smith's moral directives, a housewife says, "She sometimes tells you of selfish people in the world we live in and how wrong it is." From all this emerges a simplified system of moral accounting through which her fans, perhaps laboring under a burdensome routine, may come to regard themselves with some satisfaction. They have, at least, the moral profits of their virtues.

No Counterpropaganda

We have yet to consider why the Smith public images have found such widespread acceptance. To be sure, she has a daily hearing for her social roles and this aids the diffusion of her self-portraits. But, above all, it should be noted that these images are at no point systematically challenged. Once she has captured the attention of her large audience, there are none to counteract "consumer acceptance" of these images. There are relatively few celebrities in this strategic position. Political leaders must share radio time with the opposition who may directly dispute their views and self-descriptions. Not so with Smith. Of course, she has competitors in the market of radio advertising, but none who set themselves to question what she has said. Kenneth Burke has observed this pattern in more general terms: ". . . businessmen compete with one another by trying to *praise their own commodity* more persuasively than their rivals, whereas politicians compete by slandering *the opposition*. When you add it all up, you get a grand total of absolute praise for business and a grand total of absolute slander for politics."[12]

Linking herself with the cardinal American values, Smith establishes a series of public images which are at no point subject to a counterpropaganda. In this restricted sense, she monopolizes public imagination.[13] Accounts of her generosity are set afloat, and no opposition group challenges her motives, as would be the case with a rival political candidate. The portrait of Smith-the-mother-figure is systematically fostered, and it is in no one's interest to question its appropriateness. The impression she creates, if it is not criticized by the listener himself, goes undisturbed. It is one-way suggestion, not unlike that of the hypnotist whose suggestions to the subject are unopposed.

The organization of American radio permits the building of a public figure who can be utilized for purposes of mass persuasion. Whether this influence is to be exercised for good or for ill continues to be largely a decision vested in the directors of radio networks and stations.

[12] Kenneth Burke, *Attitudes toward History* (New York, 1937), Vol. II, p. 197.

[13] On the "monopolistic" character of certain types of radio programs, see Paul F. Lazarsfeld, "The Effects of Radio on Public Opinion," in Douglas Waples, editor, *Print, Radio and Film in a Democracy* (Chicago: University of Chicago Press, 1942), pp. 74–76.

I'm crazy about my daytime show. If I had to choose between singing and talking, I'd give up the singing. I'm just fascinated by the power of speech. That day of bond-selling proved it to me.

—Kate Smith, *in a published interview*

Do you know that in the first war she was only a kid and she stood on a soapbox and sang for the soldiers. She does the same thing now. I heard it over the radio not long ago. She was talking with the man on her program and she said, remember when I was only a kid and sang for the soldier boys. She sang 'Over There' and all those kinda songs. *I'll bet they'll make a book of her—something everyone can read about, what she's done.* I think she's done good things for other people.

—A housewife, *in an unpublished interview*

The possibilities for good and evil here are immense: the secondary personal contact with voice and image may increase the amount of mass regimentation, all the more because the opportunity for individual members reacting directly upon the leader himself, as in a local meeting, becomes farther and farther removed.

—Lewis Mumford, *Technics and Civilization*

Chapter 7

MASS PERSUASION: A TECHNICAL PROBLEM AND A MORAL DILEMMA

THE POWER of speech, which so fascinates Kate Smith that she threatens to doff the feathers of a songbird for the mantle of an orator, is no simple faculty lodged in the person of a persuasive speaker. This much is clear from our inquiry into a minor episode of mass persuasion. The over-all strategy of persuasion made use of a special social situation in which mass interest and emotions were centered on a national co-operative venture. Varied techniques and devices were employed to move the audience from a state of mind to definite action. But, as has been intimated throughout our study, these devices of mass persuasion, primarily *technical* in character though they are, have a *moral* dimension as well. In adopting the standpoint of the technician, we are interested only in questions of what proved effective and how it came to be so. From the standpoint of the citizen, we want to raise questions of a broader social and moral nature. Yet the technical and moral implications are in fact closely interlaced and do not permit us the convenient splitting of our personality into the technician and the citizen selves. The techniques employed in mass persuasion have direct social implications and a code of morals immediately limits the choice of effective techniques.

The Technical Dimension

Perhaps the most general finding of our inquiry is the con-figurative or patterned nature of this episode of mass persuasion. The elements which entered into this pattern extend far beyond the gross emotional symbols employed by Smith. This was no simple event in which the use of the "correct appeals" alone served to persuade large numbers of people. To have confined our inquiry to the content of what Smith said would have been to overlook the more general pattern of persuasion. The analysis of this content alone provides only a limited clue to what proved persuasive and it is, at best, inevitably thin, partly misleading and seriously incomplete. "Copy slants," as the phrasings are called by those versed in the arts of commercial persuasion, were an integral but not decisive part of the total event.

The general finding that it was not only what Smith had to say that furthered persuasion led to the observation that other effective components of her campaign had been fashioned before the day of the marathon. The process of persuasion was well under way before she began her daylong exhortations. To ignore this fact by focusing solely on her appeals during the marathon would be to lose sight of integral phases of the campaign.

Likely to be neglected, if only because it is so obvious, is the important role played by the war itself, with the shared sentiments and values that it brought about. Expressing and partly shaping these sentiments was the continuing flow of appeals, pronouncements and facts broadcast through radio, print, film, and word of mouth, all dealing with the central place of war bonds as a civilian contribution to a national effort. To a large extent, of course, Smith rode the crest of this wave. Her appeals were carried along by an upsurge of common motivations and interests. She had, so to speak, a vast emotional capital on which to draw for her own bond drive.

Similarly antedating the marathon were the public images of Smith, themselves the product of years of sedulous attention to the building of a public reputation. The effectiveness of what she had to say cannot be dissociated from these public images. She had long since become identified as a patriot nonpareil, at once a leader and, in words broadcast by ex-Governor Al Smith during the fourth drive, "one of the little people of America." It was this imagery, antedating the bond drive and reinforced by it, that could lead devoted followers to rally round their idol and lay their bond pledges upon the altar of their devotion. It was this imagery, also, that permitted the bond pledge to become simultaneously an expression of their fealty to Smith and to their country. She had long been for many an object of loyalty, a public figure who stood beyond conflicting group interests, who espoused nothing but the undebated virtues and the sacred symbols. The prevalence of these images testifies to the powerful role of publicity in a mass society. (It will be remembered that although fourteen of approximately a thousand New Yorkers had never heard of the ex-presidential candidate Wendell Willkie, only one could not identify the radio singer Kate Smith.) And, as we have seen, the appeals typically expressed by Smith were carefully tailored to her public images.

If the fusion of sentiments brought on by the war and the carefully nurtured reputation of Smith were indispensable preconditions, the technique of the marathon itself contributed further to her effectiveness. For it was not only what she *said* but what she *did* during the marathon that enhanced persuasion. The public sacrifice presumably entailed by a daylong stint at the microphone set Smith apart from others who "only talked but didn't act." Propaganda of the deed proved persuasive among some who rejected propaganda of the word. Listeners who revealed their profound distrust of the "power of speech" were moved by the symbolic act.

It was within this context—a concert of effort motivated by

the war, a kaleidoscopic set of public images of Smith and the tactics of the marathon—that Smith's appeals took effect. The context supplied cogency to words which might otherwise have been less than persuasive. But once this context was provided, the choice of appeals and their precise formulation became decisive in affecting the degree of mass persuasion. This seems to be shown by the enormous increase of pledges obtained by Smith in her fourth bond drive which followed by some months the drive we have been examining. The thirty-nine millions of pledges in the third grew to a hundred and ten millions in the fourth all-day drive. A few excerpts from the Smith broadcasts in the latter marathon will show how technicians in the management of public opinion come to develop more "effective" appeals.

Technicians in Sentiment

At various points in our study we have noted types of audience reaction which indicated that the Smith appeals were less effective than they might otherwise have been. Some of her themes elicited a counterreaction. For example, her exclusive appeal to sentiment antagonized some listeners who defined the purchase of bonds as a "rational investment." So, too, she failed to quicken the interest of male listeners who felt that her appeals were directed primarily to women. In other instances we found that she had not directly appealed to certain prevalent sentiments—e.g., that it would profane a sacred obligation to accept special premiums for the purchase of a bond. These technical flaws in the third bond drive are selected precisely because Smith's script writers obviously sought to remedy them in her next drive. They thus permit us to see how technicians apply their skills to the persuasion of large sectors of the population.

By early evening, when the male folk had presumably returned home from work, Smith began to address broadcasts explicitly to them. Plainly, she wished to capture the "rationalists" in the male audince, a sector which had apparently been largely unmoved by her previous bond drives. The tactics employed in these broadcasts are revealing. If she wished to motivate those listeners who looked upon war bonds primarily as a secure investment, one might suppose that she would address herself directly to the war-bonds-as-safe-investments theme, so often used in the national bond campaigns. But this is precisely what she avoided. For, as we have seen, a direct financial appeal would be out of character for Smith. To preserve intact the public image of Smith-the-moralist and yet to reach the group who heretofore had defined bonds in terms of secular investments, her script writers employed a complex of delicately interlaced techniques. It will be instructive to follow these techniques in detail if we are to understand the careful maneuvers of these tacticians in public sentiment.

Smith opened the broadcasts to men with a forthright personal statement of an observation which was disturbing her, at once allaying any impression that she intended to criticize her male listeners.

> "Now, I'd like to talk to the men. Oh, you men have been sending in your orders too. I don't mean that, but I've got something on my mind that concerns the men of this nation and I'd like to talk it over."

Having struck this keynote of candor in which she is about to engage in a heart-to-heart talk, she at once launched into a reported indictment of men who purchase bonds in the spirit of a calculating investor. Her listeners, of course, knew that the morally superior motivation for the purchase of war bonds is that of disinterested moral obligation. They knew that war bonds are primarily sacred rather than secular, that they are symbols of consecrated national purpose rather than merely smart investments. Smith's description of the portrait of the calculating investor presumably set in train feelings of guilt and shame among those who recognized the portrait as something of a self-likeness. Smith etched the portrait in acid:

> "*It's been said* that listeners who pride themselves on being rational don't phone in pledges for bonds because they feel such a purchase is the result of emotional pressure. *I've been told* that to men, buying bonds is a form of business, that it's handled like a business deal. *I've been told* that men buy their bonds through banks. Oh yes, *some of these people say,* 'Men like to hear Kate Smith sing songs, but when she tries to play on their emotions and begs them to buy just one more bond, they balk. Because bond-buying is the result of planning ahead, the result of budgeting and bookkeeping. Bond-buying is a careful considered investment, not to be undertaken at the sound of a voice, at the stories of atrocities committed on American boys who are prisoners of the Japanese, American boys lying in hospitals, wounded and maimed. That's emotionalism.'"

This juxtaposition of the cold-blooded, utilitarian investor and American boys wounded and maimed presumably provoked acute feelings of guilt, self-blame and unworthiness among those who detected in her description something more than an unfounded caricature of themselves. But throughout, it will be noted, this indictment stemmed not from Smith herself, but from others. ("It's been said . . . " "I've been told . . ." "Some of these people say . . .") She was merely reporting a series of "charges" which impugn the moral character of the American man at home. Only then, having stimulated anew a sense of inner conflict among her listeners, did Smith take up her own position. And, in accord with her public role as a mother figure, she rejected the out-group of "critics" and identified herself with her male listeners:

"Yes, that's what *they* say, *some of these wise people* who know only the world of dollars and cents, profit and loss, the jingle of the cash register, the cold figures in a bank book. That's what they say and gentlemen, I tell you now, *I* . . . *DON'T* . . . *BELIEVE* . . . *IT! I say THEY LIE,* these people who think our American businessmen don't like emotionalism, don't harbor sentiment in their hearts."

This indignant rejection of the implied criticism, this reaffirmation of faith in the American male character, erased the occasion for self-blame. Smith-the-mother-figure provided reassurance. For those who experienced moral conflict, she gave moral succor. She allied herself confidently with American men everywhere, in the market place, the workshop and the office, asserting her conviction that the occasion for conflict was seeming rather than real. These men had it in them to see the right and to do the right. There was no need for guilt, for she had ready proof that they had only lofty motives, immune from attack by themselves or by others. And in all this Smith reinforced the claims of moral obligation. In this battle of motives, she sided with the Superego against the Ego.

"I say they lie, because these businessmen, these factory workers, these office employees, these older men who are doing a job at home are Americans, and coming closer to their homes and their hearts, they're the fathers of these sons for whom I'm working today."

And then, lest complacency set in, she reinforced the dictates of conscience in a crescendo of sacrosanct symbols:

"They are the fathers of these splendid boys who have gone into battle, not because they liked war, not because they had any inner urge to bomb and kill and destroy, not because they yearned to leave the little town or the big city that was home. They went because of the ideals, and sentiment, and love of country. They went for the highest motives that young men can have, the same motives that sent you, their Dads, to war, in 1917: the willingness to give their lives to keep a free America free, and to bring new freedom, new blessed peace to enslaved countries across the sea. They went because little children were being bombed as they recited their lessons in school, or as they sang their hymns in church on Sunday. They went because they felt that burning inner urge to fight for the right."

And having once again activated feelings of guilt and remorse, Smith built an easy road to atonement. The purchase of a war bond, more specifically the purchase of a bond from Smith who rejects out of hand the notion that bonds may also serve one's narrowly defined self-interest, such an act would testify beyond all question to one's moral integrity. An immediate symbolic act would wash away all semblance of guilt and shame.

"Nobody can tell me their fathers here at home aren't bursting with pride. Nobody can tell me that they can sit down coolly and separate sentiment,—emotionalism, if you want to call it that—from bond-buying. Nobody can tell me that it's just a matter of bookkeeping or planned investment, when they lay those invasion dollars on the line. . . . How about you, Mr. America? Are you going to count the cost, and add up careful investments, and do planned bookkeeping when our kids overseas have some accounts of their own to balance—to balance in blood. How about you? Will you listen to your heart—now?"

This intricate pattern of Smith's initial reinforcement of inner conflicts and of her confident support of the "higher" motives of disinterested moral obligation followed by the suggestion that the purchase of a bond from Smith would wipe out all sense of self-humiliation—this pattern of appeals, new to her fourth bond drive, presumably served its purpose. For in a later broadcast, Smith could go on to say:

"Just a little while ago, I spoke to the fathers of America, the

American Dads who back in 1917 went off to war, just as their fine sons are doing today. I said that some people were saying that our American men didn't buy bonds on the spur of the moment—just like that. They were not ruled by sentiment. And I said—I didn't believe it. *I said my little say, and you American Dads from coast to coast answered, answered from your heart, just as I knew in my heart that you would. You're still answering, your orders are still pouring in.* They're riding across the land in proud procession, adding up the dollars, putting the cash on the line, to make a pathway for your sons to march on to victory, and to come home to peace. Thank you—thank you. We've got not one but two backbones to this nation . . . The Dads of 1917, and the sons of 1944."

The reference to the twin backbones of the nation was not only a peculiar anatomical trope; it was a figure of speech which helped bind together the earlier and later broadcasts which made up this marathon. For earlier in the day ex-Governor Smith had made it clear that Kate Smith too was numbered among those who are "the backbone of the nation."

"We don't think of you, Kate, as an impressive personality, or the Queen of the Air, or anything like that. We think of you as plain Kate Smith, as one of the little people of America, and when I say that, I mean one of the average, everyday folks who, incidentally, are the backbone of the nation. It's the plain, average everyday kids from the little towns who are winning this war. It's the average everyday Americans at home who are winning this war. It's the average everyday Americans at home who are piling up these tremendous bond sales. . . . You reach those people because you are those people . . ."

And drawing upon this image of plain Kate Smith, the script writers introduced another theme largely absent from the previous bond drive. We found, it will be remembered, that fully half of a cross section of a thousand New Yorkers expe-

rienced a conflict between the secular and the sacred aspects
of war bonds and that they viewed special prizes and "bonuses"
for the purchase of a bond as virtually profaning a moral obligation. ("You don't sell your patriotism—that's how I feel...")
Still representing the national superego, so to speak, Smith
assailed the conscience of those who require special inducements to pledge a bond: •

> "I'm just a plain simple American, with a plain, simple,
> straightforward message. I'm no glamour personality who
> offers you a flower from my hair, who promises you an auto-
> graph, or a picture, or a souvenir booklet. This is no Bingo
> game we're playing. And I don't think you want any of these
> things. I think you want what I want, what our men over-
> seas want, what one hundred and thirty million Americans
> want. We want to get this war over ..."

These few instances from the fourth bond drive are perhaps
sufficient to suggest the tactics of the technicians in sentiment.
They never lose sight of the prevailing images of Smith. Only
those appeals are used which are consistent with these images,
thus serving not only to elicit the desired bond pledge but also
to reinforce these images anew. The appeal to narrow self-
interest, for example, could not be part of Smith's grammar of
motives. It would seriously conflict with the public character
to which her script writers give studied expression. Within the
vocabulary of purpose which is consistent with her public
character, however, script writers have a wide range of choice.
Typically, they seek out sources of guilt and inner conflict
among her listeners and direct their thrusts toward these areas
of moral vulnerability. Having reinforced the conflict, they
at once suggest a ready solution. To say, therefore, that they
appeal to sentiment is to be something less than adequate. Their
techniques can be more precisely defined. By utilizing the tensions between disinterested moral obligation and narrow self-

interest, they motivate the listener to follow their suggestion. An immediate act promises surcease from moral conflict. And through the generous use of sacred symbols, invulnerable to attack, they ally Smith with national pieties.

The Moral Dimension

Our primary concern with the social psychology of mass persuasion should not obscure its moral dimension. The technician or practitioner in mass opinion and his academic counterpart, the student of social psychology, cannot escape the moral issues which permeate propaganda as a means of social control. The character of these moral issues differs somewhat for the practitioner and the investigator, but in both cases the issues themselves are inescapable.

The practitioner in propaganda is at once confronted by a dilemma: he must either forego the use of certain techniques of persuasion which will help him obtain the immediate end-in-view or violate prevailing moral codes. He must choose between being a less than fully effective technician and a scrupulous human being or an effective technician and a less than scrupulous human being. The pressure of the immediate objective tends to push him toward the first of these alternatives.[1] For when effective mass persuasion·is sought, and when "effectiveness" is measured solely by the number of people who can be brought to the desired action or the desired frame of mind, then the choice of techniques of persuasion will be governed by a narrowly technical and amoral criterion. And this criterion exacts a price of the prevailing morality, for it expresses a manipulative attitude toward man and society. It inevitably pushes toward the use of whatsoever techniques "work."

[1] R. K. Merton, "Social Structure and Anomie," *Amer. Soc. Review*, 1938, 3, 672–82.

The sense of power that accrues to manipulators of mass opinion, it would appear, does not always compensate for the correlative sense of guilt. The conflict may lead them to a flight into cynicism. Or it may lead to uneasy efforts to exonerate themselves from moral responsibility for the use of manipulative techniques by helplessly declaring, to themselves and to all who will listen, that "unfortunately, that's the way the world is. People are moved by emotions, by fear and hope and anxiety, and not by information or knowledge." It may be pointed out that complex situations must be simplified for mass publics and, in the course of simplification, much that is relevant must be omitted. Or, to take the concrete case we have been examining, it may be argued that the definition of war bonds as a device for curbing inflation is too cold and too remote and too difficult a conception to be effective in mass persuasion. It is preferable to focus on the sacred and sentimental aspects of war bonds, for this "copy slant" brings "results."

Like most half-truths, the notion that leaders of mass opinion must traffic in sentiment has a specious cogency. Values *are* rooted in sentiment and values *are* ineluctably linked with action. But the whole-truth extends beyond this observation. Appeals to sentiment within the context of relevant information and knowledge are basically different from appeals to sentiment which blur and obscure this knowledge. Mass persuasion is not manipulative when it provides access to the pertinent facts; it is manipulative when the appeal to sentiment is used to the exclusion of pertinent information.

The technician, then, must decide whether or not to use certain techniques which though possibly "effective" violate his own sentiments and moral codes. He must decide whether or not he should devise techniques for exploiting mass anxieties, for using sentimental appeals in place of information, for masking private purpose in the guise of common purpose.[2] He faces the moral problem of choosing not only among social ends but also among propaganda means.

Although less conspicuous and less commonly admitted, a comparable problem confronts the social scientist investigating mass opinion. He may adopt the standpoint of the positivist, proclaim the ethical neutrality of science, insist upon his exclusive concern with the advancement of knowledge, explain that science deals only with the discovery of uniformities and not with ends and assert that in his role as a detached and dispassionate scientist, he has no traffic with values. He may, in short, affirm an occupational philosophy which appears to absolve him of any responsibility for the use to which his discoveries in methods of mass persuasion may be put. With its specious and delusory distinction between "ends" and "means" and its insistence that the intrusion of social values into the work of scientists makes for special pleading, this philosophy fails to note that the investigator's social values do influence his choice and definition of problems. The investigator may naïvely suppose that he is engaged in the value-free activity of research, whereas in fact he may simply have so defined his research problems that the results will be of use to one group

[2] During the war, imagination triumphed over conscience among advertisers who "ingeniously" related their products to the war effort. Radio commercials were not immune from this technique. A commercial dentist for example, suggests that a victory smile helps boost morale and that we çan have that smile by purchasing our dentures from him. So, too, a clothing manufacturer reminds listeners that morale is a precious asset in time of war and that smart clothes, more particularly Selfridge Lane Clothes, give a man confidence and courage. Even ice cream becomes essential to the war effort. "Expecting your boys back from an army camp? Give them JL Ice Cream. They get good food in the army and it's your job to give them the same at home." And a manufacturer of cosmetics becomes solicitous about the imbalance in the sex ratio resulting from the war. "Fewer men around because of the war? Competition keen? Keep your skin smooth. Keep attractive for the boys in the service when they come marching home." Office of Radio Research, *Broadcasting the War*, Bur. Intelligence, OWI, 1943, p. 37.

in the society, and not to others. His very choice and definition of a problem reflects his tacit values.

To illustrate: the "value-free" investigator of propaganda proceeds to the well-established mode of scientific formulations, and states his findings: "*If* these techniques of persuasion are used, *then* there will be (with a stated degree of probability) a given proportion of people persuaded to take the desired action." Here, then, is a formulation in the honored and successful tradition of science—apparently free of values. The investigator takes no moral stand. He merely reports his findings, and these, if they are valid, can be used by any interested group, liberal or reactionary, democratic or fascistic, idealistic or power-hungry. But this comfortable solution of a moral problem by the abdication of moral responsibility happens to be no solution at all, for it overlooks the crux of the problem: the initial formulation of the scientific investigation has been conditioned by the implied values of the scientst.

Thus, had the investigator been oriented toward such democratic values as respect for the dignity of the individual, he would have framed his scientific problem differently. He would not only have asked which techniques of persuasion produce the *immediate result* of moving a given proportion of people to action, but also, what are the *further, more remote* but not necessarily less significant, *effects* of these techniques upon the individual personality and the society? He would be, in short, sensitized to certain questions stemming from his democratic values which would otherwise be readily overlooked. For example he would ask, Does the unelaborated appeal to sentiment which displaces the information pertinent to assessing this sentiment blunt the critical capacities of listeners? What are the effects upon the personality of being subjected to virtual terrorization by advertisements which threaten the individual with social ostracism unless he uses the advertised defense against halitosis or B.O.? Or, more relevantly, what are the effects, in addition to increasing the sale of bonds, of terrorizing the parents of boys in military service by the threat that only through their purchase of war bonds can they ensure the safety of their sons and their ultimate return home? Do certain types of war bond drives by celebrities do more to pyramid their reputations as patriots than to further the sale of bonds which would otherwise not have been purchased? No single advertising or propaganda campaign may significantly affect the psychological stability of those subjected to it. But a society subjected ceaselessly to a flow of "effective" half-truths and the exploitation of mass anxieties may all the sooner lose that mutuality of confidence and reciprocal trust so essential to a stable social structure. A "morally neutral" investigation of propaganda will be less likely than an inquiry stemming from democratic values to address itself to such questions.

The issue has been drawn in its most general terms by John Dewey: "Certainly nothing can justify or condemn means except ends, results. But we have to include consequences impartially. . . . It is wilful folly to fasten upon some single end or consequence which is liked, and permit the view of that to blot from perception all other undesired and undesirable consequences."[3] If this study has one major implication for the understanding of mass persuasion, it consists in this recognition of the intimate interrelation of technique and morality.

[3] John Dewey, *Human Nature and Conduct* (New York: Henry Holt & Co., 1922), pp. 228–229. *Cf.* R. T. Merton, "The Unanticipated Consequences of Purposive Social Action," *American Sociological Review*, 1936, 1, 894–904.

Appendix A

THE INTERVIEW GUIDE

THE AREAS covered in the hundred intensive interviews had two sources: hypotheses in social psychology on which we wanted to throw some light and a series of preliminary case studies of listeners to the Smith bond drive. Although the interviewers were instructed to cover the entire range of areas included in the interview guide, they did not follow a fixed course of inquiry. Each informant was left free to develop most fully those aspects of the drive which loomed largest in his own experience. The careful selection of interviewers—all of whom had had intensive training in psychology and sociology—and daily conferences with the directors of the study went far toward ensuring full and accurate reporting of pertinent materials. In all instances the interview was conducted in the home of the informant. It was recorded either stenographically or in the form of brief notes and immediately thereafter expanded into its final form.

The interviewer did not ask a predetermined set of questions. Instead, he encouraged informants to describe their experiences in their own way and only toward the close of the interview, did he introduce questions from the interview guide that is here reproduced.

The brief polling interview with 978 New Yorkers was designed to check on some of the chief hypotheses stemming from the preliminary analysis of the intensive interviews. Had there been a larger number of strategic questions included in the poll, the range of confirmed findings would have been materially broadened. The cost of a more extended poll, however, was prohibitive. The field staff of The Pulse, Inc., conducted the poll; the questions are set forth in this appendix.

POLLING INTERVIEW SCHEDULE

1. If you had to choose one well-known person to sell war-bonds over the radio, which one of these would be your first choice? Last choice?

		First Choice	Last Choice
	Betty Grable	....	....
	Wendell Willkie	....	....
Order....	Kate Smith	....	....
	Frank Sinatra	....	....
	Martin Block	....	....

   A. Why is (mention first choice) your first choice? ....
   ....
   B. Why is (mention last choice) your last choice? ....
   ....
   (Instruction: Ask the *Why* immediately after first choice is given, before going on to ask who would be last choice.)
2. Do you usually buy bonds to help some person or group meet their quota? Yes...... No...... (if yes) Who? ....
3. Have you ever been given anything extra such as theatre tickets, records, books, etc., when you bought a war bond? Yes...... No......
   A. Do you think it's a good idea to give things to people who buy bonds? Yes...... No...... (if no) Why not? ....
   ....
4. Do you listen to Kate Smith's program at 12:00 o'clock noon on WABC? Regularly...... Sometimes...... Not at all......
5. If you had to describe Kate Smith, which one of these would you choose? She is: (which one of these would be your last choice?)

		First Choice	Last Choice
	Very Patriotic	....	....
	All out to help others	....	....
	An entertainer	....	....
Order...	A motherly kind of person	....	....
	Able to give advice and things to think about	....	....
	An average American woman	....	....

6. Have you ever heard Kate Smith make an all-day appeal over the radio, to buy bonds? Yes..... No..... (If yes) Have you ever ordered a bond through Kate Smith? Yes.....No.....
   A. Have you ever ordered a bond through anyone who appealed over the radio? Yes..... No..... (If yes) Who? ....
7. When Kate Smith goes on the air to sell bonds, do you feel she is thinking about the publicity she will get......, about the amount of bonds she will sell......, or both......?
Person interviewed: M.... F..... Education: Last grade or level of school completed........................
Econ. Level: A.... B.... C.... D ....Telephone Ownership: Yes... No...

Age: Under 20.... 20–29.... 30–39....40–49....50–59.... 60 & over....
Closest relative in armed services ....

Name .... Address ....

Date .... Interviewer ....

GUIDE FOR THE INTENSIVE INTERVIEW

Introductory open-ended question: Thinking back on it, what was your main impression of the Kate Smith bond drive?

1. Do you remember at what time of day you first heard Kate Smith asking people to buy bonds? How did you happen to hear her that first time?
2. How did you feel about her doing this when you first heard her?
3. Did you hear her any more during that day and evening? About how many times altogether? (Check against duration of listening.)
4. How did you find yourself picturing Kate Smith? How did she look, do you suppose? How do you think she felt about this job she was doing?
5. Did your feelings about the appeal she was making change any as she kept on broadcasting? (Note to interviewers: Was there any fluctuation in attitudes toward Smith as respondent continued listening?)
6. Did you notice any change in her while you were listening? Were you looking for any change in her?
7. At what time did you buy your bond? How many times had you heard her before you decided to buy your bond? (Reasons for lapse of time between decision to buy and the actual phone call.)
8. Do you remember what she was talking about when you made up your mind to call about a bond—the story she was telling, or anything in particular about the appeal she was making? Did this story impress you more than the others she told? Why?
9. Did you think of any reasons why you shouldn't buy a bond just then—that is, did you argue with yourself about it before you made up your mind definitely to do it? (If there were

any such reasons for delay.) What made you go ahead and buy it?

10. Did you talk it over with anyone before you bought a bond? What did you tell them? What was said at the time you decided to call?

11. Did you expect to talk to Kate Smith when you called?

12. Did you consider buying it at your bank or a store or from someone else instead of Kate Smith that day?

13. Did you think it would be easier or harder to buy it by phone than to buy it somewhere else? Or didn't this make any difference to you?

14. How would you have felt if you hadn't bought a bond just then?

15. How did you feel *after* you bought the bond? (Probes: Did you keep on listening to Kate Smith after you bought the bond? With more or less interest? Why? What were you mainly listening for then?)

16. Did you find yourself listening carefully to her different stories—or weren't they important for you? (If "listened carefully") What was there about them that interested you? (If "did not listen carefully") Why didn't you listen to them with much interest?

17. Did she repeat any of her stories or were they different each time?

18. Did you listen to the radio on that day any more, any less, or about the same amount as usual?

   (If different:) Why was that? (Probes: Did you stay tuned to the station Kate Smith was on more or less than usual? Why? Did you miss any of your regular programs?)

19. Did you keep track of the amount she was selling as the day went on? Was this of any interest to you?

20. Do you happen to know how much it was that she sold? When did you hear that? Did this interest you particularly?

21. Did you hear her mention any particular cities and how they were doing? What were your feelings about this?

22. Do you listen to Kate Smith's broadcasts at noon regularly, sometimes, never?

   What about her Friday night broadcasts?

23. What was your opinion of Kate Smith *before* her bond-selling

day? What picture did you nave of her? (Probe: What do you like most about her? What do you dislike about her?)

24. Were your feelings about her when she was broadcasting about bond-buying any different from your usual opinion of her? In what way? Why did they change?

25. Looking back on it, what would you say your *main* impression of the Kate Smith bond drive that day was? (Probe: Do you remember mostly Kate herself or what she said?)

26. Had you ever heard her broadcasting about bonds in any of the campaigns before this one?

(If yes) Did you buy a bond then? Did you consider buying?

27. What were your reactions to other requests to buy bonds in newspapers, radio, movies or elsewhere during this third drive before you heard Kate Smith? Any particular ones that you remember?

28. Had you heard other stars or important people selling bonds on the radio during this recent drive?

A. Who? Had you considered buying any bonds from them?

B. Did any of them say the same things that Kate Smith said?

C. What led you to buy from her (rather than *or* as well as) from the others?

29. Do you remember what station you were listening to when you bought the bond from Kate Smith?

30. Did you hear anyone else on the air that day talking about Kate Smith's drive to buy bonds? Any particular ones that you remember? What impressions did you get about Kate Smith from what they said?

31. What do you consider is the *main* purpose of the government's campaign to get people to buy bonds?

32. Was this bond that you bought from Kate Smith one that you bought in *addition* to the other bonds that you had bought or intended to buy, or was it one that you planned to buy anyway? (Probe for *evidence*.)

33. Do you have any regular plan for buying bonds? Where did you buy the last bond that you bought before the purchase from Kate Smith?

34. Would you say that it really cut down on money that you

would have spent on other things to buy that bond—or was it money that you intended to put into bonds anyway?

35. Who usually buys the bonds in your family—if you live with your family?

   (If someone other than respondent:) How did it happen that it was you who bought this particular bond? Did you discuss it with . . . . (usual buyer)?

36. Did you discuss buying this bond from Kate Smith with anyone afterward? What did you say?

37. Are there any reasons besides patriotic ones for buying war bonds? What?

38. Would you mind telling me what percentage of your (your family's) income goes into bonds?

39. It has been said that some people buy bonds on the spur of the moment that they can't really afford. What, do you suppose, would make people do that?

40. Do you think that there *should* be special bond drives or do you think that people should be let alone to buy as many bonds as they want to?

Attitudes:

41. Do you feel that this country would be better off or worse off if the wealth were spread more evenly among the people?

42. What do you think about this statement: In the long run, rich people are not any happier than poor people?

43. What do you think about this statement: College education may be a good thing, but after all lots of the people who get things done are not college educated.

44. Do you think moral standards in this country are too strict, not strict enough, or about right?

Personal Data:

Name .... Address ....

Sex: M.... F.... Education: Last grade or year

Age: Under 21.... of school attended

    21–30.... ....

    31–40.... Economic

    41–50.... level: A.. B.. C.. D..

    51–60.... Marital status: Married ...

    60 and Single ...

    over.... Widowed...

Occupation of Divorced...

    respondent: .... Closest relative in

Occupation of the armed forces: ....

    breadwinner: .... Telephone in the home: .....

Date of Interview: .... Name of Interviewer: ......

Appendix B

COMPOSITION OF INFORMANTS

POLL POPULATION

Sex	%
Male	29
Female	71
Total per cent	100
No. of cases	978

Age	%
Under 20	6
20–29	17
30–39	26
40–49	27
50–59	15
60 and over	8
No answer	1
Total per cent	100
No. of cases	978

Education	%
College graduate	5
Some college	5
High school graduate	35
Some high school	10
Grade school graduate	27
Some grade school	11
Trade or business school	1
No schooling	3
No answer	3
Total per cent	100
No. of cases	978

Socio-Economic Level*	%
A ("Wealthy")	5
B ("Above average")	25
C ("Average")	41
D ("Less than average")	26
No answer or don't know	2
Total per cent	100
No. of cases	978

Relatives in Armed Services	%
Immediate	41
Others	48
None	11
Total per cent	100
No. of cases	978

* For a discussion of the reliability and validity of interviewers' ratings of economic status, see Hadley Cantril, *et al.*, *Gauging Public Opinion* (Princeton University Press, 1944), Chap. VII.

INTENSIVE INTERVIEW POPULATION

Sex	%
Male	12
Female	88
No. of cases	100

Age	%
20 or less	4
21–30	21
31–40	17
41–50	26
51–60	22
Over 60	10
No. of cases	100

Education	%
College graduate	11
Some college	11
High school graduate	27
Some high school	15
Grade school graduate	24
Less than grade school	8
No answer	4
No. of cases	100

Socioeconomic Level	%
A ("Wealthy")	4
B ("Above average")	35
C ("Average")	54
D ("Less than average")	5
No answer	2
No. of cases	100

Relatives in Armed Services	%
Immediate	58
Others	32
None	7
No answer	3
No. of cases	100

Marital Status	%
Married	69
Single	16
Widowed	—
Divorced, separated	15
No. of cases	100

Telephone in Home	%
Yes	89
No	8
No answer	3
No. of cases	100

Appendix C

STATISTICAL TABLES

I. "If you had to choose one well-known person to sell war bonds over the radio, which one of these would be your first choice?" *

A. *Sex differences:*

A considerable majority of men and women alike select Smith as first choice. For notably different reasons, men accord a higher vote to Grable and Willkie, but 57 per cent nevertheless make Smith their first choice.

TABLE I-A

Sex	% Male	% Female	% Total
Betty Grable	12	5	7
Wendell Willkie	15	9	11
Kate Smith	57	64	62
Frank Sinatra	6	8	7
Martin Block	10	14	13
Total per cent	100	100	100
No. of cases	265	668	933

* This was the initial question in the poll interview, so that respondents had no clue to our particular interest in the Smith bond drive. The order of names of "candidates" was rotated in successive interviews to avoid any bias possibly resulting from the order in which they occur.

B. *Age differences:*

Although Smith was first choice among both "young" and "old," she gives ground somewhat to Block and Sinatra among the younger respondents.

TABLE I-B

Age	% Under 40	% Over 40
Betty Grable	7	7
Wendell Willkie	10	12
Kate Smith.............	56	68
Frank Sinatra	9	5
Martin Block	18	8
Total per cent	100	100
No. of cases	463	459

C. *Economic and educational level:*

Smith's appeal as a bond salesman is no respecter of income. She is selected equally often by persons on each of the three economic levels. But on each economic level, people are the more likely to vote for her the less their education. Conversely with Willkie: the vote for him increases with higher education of informants.

TABLE I-C

SOCIOECONOMIC LEVEL

"Wealthy and Average Plus"			"Average"			"Poor"	

EDUCATIONAL LEVEL

First Choice	% College	% High School*	% Less than High School	% College	% High School*	% Grammar	% College and High School†	% Grammar
Grable	4	6	10	8	9	7	7	10
Willkie	29	15	12	31	11	5	6	3
Kate Smith	55	62	68	46	53	70	56	65
Sinatra	2	5	5	—	10	12	3	10
Block	10	12	5	15	17	6	28	12
Total per cent .	100	100	100	100	100	100	100	100
No. of cases ..	58	161	66	26	184	153	82	154

* High school also includes those who have attended "Business School."

† College and High School have been combined in this instance, since there are only five persons with college education on this economic level.

D. *Differences between Smith fans and others:*

Although there is an expected tendency among fans to give Smith overwhelming precedence as a bond salesman, even those who never listen to her regular programs give her twice as many votes as the runners-up. We note here the role of publicity other than that provided by her broadcasts.

TABLE I-D
Listeners to Kate Smith's Programs

	% Regularly	% Sometimes	% Not at all
Betty Grable	5	5	12
Wendell Willkie	6	8	19
Kate Smith	80	67	43
Frank Sinatra	4	8	6
Martin Block	5	12	20
Total per cent	100	100	100
No. of cases	165	463	291

E. *Suitability of Kate Smith:*
A larger proportion of people who had actually heard Smith broadcast an all-day bond appeal voted for her than of those who had not. (Since there were no significant educational or economic differences between the two distributions, these could not operate as spurious factors.) This introduces the question whether the Smith "marathons" (1) make her seem more *suitable* for selling war bonds or (2) simply *better known* in this role. The preponderance of votes among those who had not heard her in this role, however, suggests that other sources of publicity have played a major part.

TABLE I-E
"Have you ever heard Kate Smith make an all-day bond appeal?"

	% Yes	% No
Betty Grable	6	8
Wendell Willkie	8	15
Kate Smith	70	51
Frank Sinatra	5	10
Martin Block	11	16
Total per cent	100	100
No. of cases	520	410

II. "Why is .... your first choice?"
The "symbolic fitness of Smith."

The reasons for selecting a candidate fall into four categories, the definitions of which are set forth in Chapter IV. The most frequent basis for choice is "technical": "he is a good salesman," "she has a large following," *etc.* The two notable findings, however, are (1) the comparatively large proportion of "moral" reasons for selecting Smith as "symbolically appropriate" and (2) the small importance ascribed to a comprehension of the issues, an awareness of what bonds are for, since only 27 people (23 per cent of those voting for Willkie) stated this reason.

TABLE II

Reasons for First Choice

	Betty Grable %	Wendell Willkie %	Kate Smith %	Frank Sinatra %	Martin Block %	Total %	Number
Detached, technical objective appraisal	67	45	48	59	64	52	609
Symbolic fitness .	3	17	32	—	9	23	275
Comprehension of public issues ..	—	23	—	—	—	2	27
Personal relation	20	10	16	32	25	18	208
Miscellaneous ...	10	5	4	9	2	5	53
No. of reasons (= 100%) .	73	119	744	78	158		1,172
No. of informants	66	101	578	67	121		933

III. *"Who would be your last choice?"*

Even more striking than Smith's precedence as first choice is the fact that so few place her last. She has, one might say, many friends and no enemies. A political figure such as Willkie, on the other hand, who has had to take a stand on many public issues obtained "first" votes from 11 per cent and "last" votes from 28 per cent. Sinatra and Grable are rejected as "inappropriate" and "ineffective" for this type of activity; Block because many people do not know him.

TABLE III

Last Choice	%
Betty Grable	16
Wendell Willkie	28
Kate Smith	3
Frank Sinatra	35
Martin Block	18
Total per cent	100
No. of cases	844

IV. "When Kate Smith goes on the air to sell war bonds, do you feel she is thinking about the publicity she will get, about the amount of bonds she will sell or both?"

Ascription of motives to Smith:
Four out of five persons feel that Smith is exclusively concerned with the sale of war bonds. This conviction becomes the more frequent the more often people listen to Smith. Even in the absence of any direct experience of Smith, however, one is likely to be convinced of her sincerity in the bondselling situation, since 78 per cent of those who never listen to her programs express this attitude.

TABLE IV

	Regularity of Listening to the Smith Noonday Program		
	Regu-larly %	Some-times %	Never %
Interested in bonds only ...	94	82	78
Interested in publicity too ..	6	18	22
Total per cent	100	100	100
No. of cases	166	479	289

V. "Do you think it is a good idea to give things to people who buy bonds?"

Taboo on profaning a "sacred" obligation:
There is a complete division of attitude toward the belief that offering "premiums" or "bonuses" for the purchase of a war bond smacks of the "immoral" since it is a patriotic obligation to buy bonds in any event. But Smith fans are slightly more likely to adopt this belief than are those who are not regular listeners to her program.

TABLE V

Should premiums be given?	Regularity of Listening to Smith Noonday Program		
	Regularly %	Occasionally or Never %	Total %
Yes	46	52	51
No	54	48	49
Total per cent	100	100	100
No. of cases	168	790	958

Index

DATE DUE

ILL 2-21-86			
GAYLORD			PRINTED IN U.S.A.